Idaho

Exposure

Marcia Katerndahl

DEDICATION

For my husband Dean and son Casey –
you are at the heart of my life.

*Two youngsters were busy digging their way to China
when some older boys came by and scoffed at them – telling
them they'd never reach their goal. After a moment's hesitation,
one of the boys replied as he held up a muddy jar full
of worms and bugs and plants,
"Yeah, but look what we've found along the way!"
~ Author Unknown*

CONTENTS

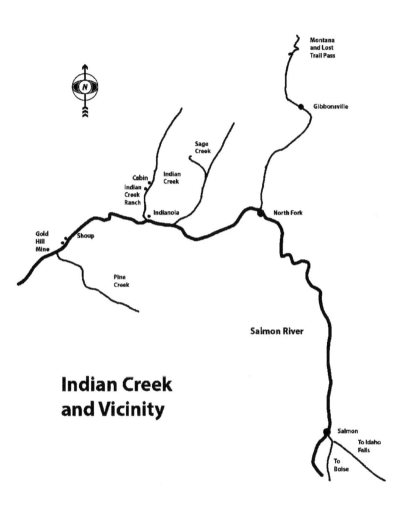

Montana
and Lost
Trail Pass

Gibbonsville

Sage
Creek

Cabin
Indian
Creek

Indian
Creek
Ranch

Indianola

North Fork

Gold
Hill
Mine

Shoup

Pine
Creek

Salmon River

Salmon

To Idaho
Falls

To
Boise

Indian Creek
and Vicinity

FORWARD

From the time my son Casey was quite small, he asked me to write about the five years his father and I lived in a remote region of Idaho surrounded by the Frank Church-Salmon River of No Return Wilderness Area, a region designated for preservation in its natural condition. Whether known to him or not, he'd asked me to share a time that led to the greatest turning point in my life.

In response to his request, yes, I do believe it's time to share that adventure from my perspective. His father, Bernie, has already written an engrossing book about that period; however, it's from a male's perspective. And as you might imagine, a wilderness existence invites the male psyche to test itself. From what I witnessed, most men love the challenges and learning curve required to survive – packing into the back country by horse and mule train for long stays; hunting one's own meat and dressing it out; felling, hauling, and chopping massive amounts of firewood for the winter's store. I could go on, but that's the gist of it. However, from my perspective – a female one – it was a steeper learning curve – one that I'm forever grateful that I ultimately embraced. At first it had more to do with adjusting to the remoteness of our location. Any romanticized view of our new life in the West was quickly struck down after we moved into our humble cabin; I felt as if the last vestiges of the moorings attached to my former life had been slashed. However, I did eventually reach a turning point which happened as I gradually immersed myself in the region and allowed myself to become a part of its fabric. The first rays of confidence came from the skills required to become integral to the Forest Service's Tree Marking Crew and then the Stand Exam Crew; and in the process, I gained lifelong female friends. Once that foundation was established, I was then able to appreciate the adventure that we had chosen rather than be overwhelmed by it. I reveled in the fiercely independent souls this remote region produced – their nonconformity, if you will. Also, living amongst animals in their world, not ours, made any preconceptions as to what might be in store each day worthless. Hence it cleared the last remnants of the cobweb-like filters from my eyes and enabled me to greet this new world with a sense of wonder rather than fear.

Even though I was in my early thirties, I know that my parents were tremendously concerned about me the entire time I lived in Idaho. And I can well understand it, especially now that I am a parent. Here their daughter had a perfectly good job and had just purchased her own home only to throw it all off and move to a wilderness area with no promised employment in sight. However, the wonderful friends I made, comical experiences I had, breathtaking sights and challenges I encountered during that time made me into who I am today – and for that I am forever grateful. I have absolutely no regrets.

~

Be it known that in a few cases out of deference to their privacy, I only used the first name of individuals. In other cases where full names seemed appropriate but I had failed to obtain their permissions before they passed on, I changed their first and/or last names. In the case of Jack and Lois and their daughter, Theresa, they had asked me for many years to write such a book. My only regret is that they are not here to read it.

Salmon River at Indianola just above where it meets Indian Creek

FIRST MONTH

Overwhelmed with loneliness during my first month up Indian Creek Canyon, I felt as if the reality of all I had left behind – and the magnitude of the challenges ahead – were suffocating the life out of me. Bernie had obtained a seasonal job with the U.S. Forest Service at the Salmon Ranger Station and received notice shortly after our arrival in mid-April that he was to join the reforestation crews a few weeks later and would be camping out during the week. Hence, I found myself alone surrounded by wilderness four days and nights each week.

Days before our arrival, we had loaded the last of the contents of the small Olathe, Kansas house I had purchased and renovated as a single person during the preceding year. As we pulled away, my pent up regrets poured out. *I hope we like it in Idaho because I like my little house and I like my little friends and I like my little job.* Had it now only been a year? So much had happened during that time – it seemed a lifetime ago.

When I looked back at my former life, I had to wonder if I still was the same person that had so confidently managed the housing rehabilitation programs for the City of Olathe and the very same person who had negotiated a personal loan with a local lending institution, which included not only the purchase of her house but also the financing for the complete renovation of it – the first such loan of its kind for that institution. My position with the city had required a person who was insightful, creative, quick-witted, and a resolute negotiator, hand-holder and facilitator. My private life had consisted of friends I felt connected with and a Labrador by the name of Lady, who shared my love of wandering about the countryside. My abode had all the makings of a dollhouse in the Arts and Crafts style. It stood up straight, was solid – simply needing a thorough face-lift. It was 735 square feet, had fourteen windows, hardwood floors and vaulted ceilings. It sat on an acre of land graced by a canopy of tall oak trees and was backed by a horse pasture. I was thirty, coming into my own, attractive, and had been called charming by some. Looking back now at that brief moment in time, I had been perfectly content with my life.

Only days after I had settled into my new home in Olathe, I began losing my bearings. Ever the romantic, I met someone and I fell in love. Bernie and I were married four months later and spent our honeymoon in the region of North Fork, Idaho, rafting the Salmon River and lodging downriver from that eye-blink of a town, at Indian Creek Guest Ranch with the owners, Jack and Lois.

After our return home, we found out that a cabin located a mile up the canyon from Indian Creek Ranch was available for lease. Jack and Lois were drawn to Bernie and me, encouraging us – offering their assistance if we wished to move there. It all seemed preordained, one event after another sweeping us along. It must be right I thought; it must be part of God's plan for my life. This was an opportunity offered to few. How could we pass it up? Fears of bears and coping with isolation were tradeoffs I would eventually overcome. We gave our notices at work six months in advance and viewed every wilderness movie which came along – and there were many. *Mother Earth News* magazine was at its peak as was anything championing getting back to nature. It seemed we were set apart, our friends standing in awe of us. (Looking back, I realize that it was the men in our immediate sphere who championed our move, not the women.) This was something Bernie and I had separately always wanted to do but practicality (a good word, one to reconcile oneself with before embarking on any great adventure) and lack of opportunity had kept our dreams at bay – until now. Now we were the courageous ones I believed – we were actually dropping out of the rat race.

It was like being swept along on a current, smoothly avoiding all the obstacles, the way being laid open at every bend, having my senses filled with a combination of expectation, hope, trepidation and excitement all the while believing in my heart that a gentle hand was guiding us along. Again, it must be all preordained. I gave myself completely and utterly to that trust. Then to suddenly be deposited up a remote canyon, alone, cut-off from all that I had loved and found familiar – I had arrived in Idaho and our new home – a remote humble two-room cabin built in the 1920's (until a month before our arrival was inhabited by mammoth wood rats), situated in a narrow canyon surrounded on every side by the steep timbered walls of National Forest land.

Drenching rain, low slung clouds and swollen creeks at our elevation was the constancy of the entire month Bernie was camped out. I had no phone, no TV, no friend near at hand – new acquaintances, but no friends. If I wished to phone anyone, I either hiked a mile to the guest ranch or drove fourteen miles up the Salmon River to the North Fork Store. The pay phone was situated next to restrooms and gas pumps, thus abounding in noise from car and human traffic. If I chose to use Jack and Lois's antique wall-mounted phone, it necessitated my cranking its handle round and round in order to be connected to an operator located in Salmon. After the operator answered, I had to talk loudly into the mouth piece requesting her to dial the number for me. My party may or may not be home after all that and, being 1981, it was before most people had answering machines. If by luck they were home, it was impossible for Jack and Lois to accord me any privacy unless they went outdoors. Also, there were twenty-two families on the party line, some finding the temptation to eavesdrop impossible to resist. Given those circumstances, I never felt comfortable enough to pour my heart out to friends or family back home. Plus, I had left them with such high hopes. So I began writing letters to anyone who seemed vaguely interested in my whereabouts. I decided out of pride and deference to those who cared to put up a brave front, all the while feeling a kind of desperate hollowness, questioning myself on every front. What had possessed me to come here? I had cut myself off from the outside world and everything I held dear. All external props that I had taken for granted – friends, family, a job – were gone.

It was during those isolated first months that I began to get to know Lois and came to love our visits over hot tea. Lois having her own set of events to mourn and reconcile, I became her confidante and she became my anchor, though she did not know it at the time.

Out of necessity with no phone line as yet connecting our two properties, Lois would show up unexpectedly at our cabin with three dogs and two cats in tow. They made quite an entourage hiking up the canyon: Nappy, a 130 lb. German Shepard; Mickey, a poodle who refused to play his assigned part; and Fang (according to Lois), their 107 year old Chihuahua, with no teeth and monstrous breath. The family cat was called Jed and their feral cat was named Spitfire.

Upon Lois's arrival, I would light a fire in the wood cook stove and put on some water for tea. I quickly learned to always have munchies on hand, such as cookies or pie, because it was such a treat to have guests. You wanted them to feel welcome and wish to stay. With the fire crackling in the background and its warm glow pervading the room, Lois and I would sit at my kitchen table sipping tea from my good china, eating treats, gazing out the window at the tunnel of green canyon hillsides, whiling away an hour or so chatting and laughing. What a delight she was and in time I would learn of her proud invincible spirit. She was a living example of any advice she gave. Even though she has since passed away, I still carry pieces of her wisdom within my heart – the main one being, *Keep your chin up, Marcia.* I have put that into practice throughout my life, understanding the hard-won place from which it came.

My new home up Indian Creek, affectionately called "John's Cabin"

Lady & me in front of our cabin

INITIATION

When Bernie and I first arrived at Indian Creek, my sense of isolation from all the external props i.e., close friends and family, a job I had been deeply committed to, neighbors close at hand, a home – my first – television, telephone etc., was profound. The unknown and seemingly boundless forest loomed on every side of our cabin, especially at night – it was DARK. And a person such as me, grown used to urban living, was ill-equipped to deal with the imaginings this produced within. To say that it gave me pause is an understatement, situating itself in the core of my being. *Breathe, Marcie, breathe,* the circular mantra in my head. Our Labrador, Lady, who used to explore open fields, hedge rows and creek beds with abandon on the outskirts of the city, now was watchful, senses on full alert, was unable or unwilling to move. She, as overwhelmed as I was, retreated to her primal bearings. I, having spent a lifetime metamorphosing from small town girl to city dweller had, or so it seemed, not the thinnest thread of resources to draw upon and was left with the one emotion I detest dealing with most: fear – pure and pervasive.

Found within my former life, the urban life, I had a sense of control over my surroundings, and if things got out of hand, there was always 911. But here in these alien environs the possible scenarios were boundless – a bear or mountain lion or rattlesnake at every turn – my mind knew no limit. Being without a phone, I lacked even the means to dial for help, and it would have been pointless to shout – no one would have heard my pleas anyway. Eventually, we did string a mile of line for a crank phone, tree to tree crisscrossing the mountain road, between our cabin and the ranch. But during that first summer and fall, other than an occasional truck laboring up the canyon, our cabin was cut off from the outside world. My initial fledgling attempt at providing myself with some sense of security when walking the canyon road or hiking the ridge behind our cabin was to attach small bells to Lady and myself – the idea being that any animals, especially bears, would hear us coming and promptly depart the area. This seemed to work because I had no chance encounters with wild warm-blooded creatures until I did away with the bells.

Strangely enough, even more than my dread of the animals was a fear of an intrusive visit from a stranger, not knowing their intentions, and having no means to defend myself if necessary, and Lady of course being of no help. She was, after all, a Labrador. I decided to ask Jack during one of his neighborly visits up the canyon. He would show up for any number of reasons – whether it be giving his dudes a little break or taking advantage of the nice breeze coming out of the mine shaft behind our cabin – it didn't matter to me – I needed his expert help.

I said, "Jack, what do I do if someone pulls up and crosses the footbridge toward the cabin? I don't want to unlock the door and they could break it down quite easily anyway. And I can't phone you or Lois."

Jack looked at me seriously, "Marcie, I tell ya what ya do. Ya get yer shotgun and ya cradle it in the crick of yer arm like so, step out the front door and say, 'State yer business, Mister!' And then, ya spit!"

Dumbfounded, "Jack, I'm serious!"

"Why, don't ya think that would pull him up short?"

"Yes, but…"

He said, "Marcie, if he doesn't stop, all ya have to do is raise yer shotgun. Ya don't have to be a marksman – that's the beauty of it. And the fella coming across that bridge will know it too!"

All this was said with a little smile. He was having fun with me and I doubled over in giggles; the thought of me, shotgun in hand, saying, "State yer business, Mister," then spitting, was too much.

So this was the beginning of my initiation into life in the West. And the message came across loud and clear, *Relax, you're going to learn to live by your wits and you'll handle it.* It was akin to the western version of tough love. And in time I came to realize how true that message was. Living in such close proximity to nature amongst those who were possessed by this remote region, I never knew what adventure I might happen upon each new day. But there was no doubt by day's end, a treasure was in store for those who could lay aside with their weary bones the struggles of the day and recall with blessed gratitude the brief encounters with a world full of wonder and abounding stories: a glimpse of a spotted fawn in a moss laden spring bed, eyes transfixed on yours; being greeted by a magnificent young bull moose standing steps from your front door, only to meld into the forest before you could even catch your breath; or to watch a sole swan driven by instinct year upon year return to a cove along the Salmon River it had once shared with its life's mate.

Sometime stories would frustrate the heart however. An elderly couple who had spent a lifetime turning a hitherto barren spot of earth leased from the Forest Service into an abundant site – fruit-laden trees, thriving flowers and vegetables enough to dry, can and store for the winter – only to be told in their seventieth years they would have to move in order that their cabin could be burned and the site returned to the forest. One was left to ask – why then? The Forest Service couldn't wait until the couple passed on? These were some of the backdrops for the adventures and heartbreaks which would greet me, teach me, christen me.

The modern world with its soul-numbing pace and unquenchable appetite for external modes of entertainment had not reached her tentacles into this enclave. And owing to an inner call too arresting to disregard, I found my life gradually intertwining with those whose very existence was in part due to their recognition that in order to survive here, one must deal with its elements head-on and recognize their dependency on one another. Some embraced it, adjusting to its limitations; some became broken by its unforgiving nature, while others eternally cursed it, yet stayed. And so with faint heart, I unwittingly came to be a disciple of its ways, and the lessons learned have graced my life since.

That's me splitting firewood

JACK AND LOIS

Sometimes people enter one's life in the form of humble everyday beings; it is not until they are gone that we are given a chance to assess their influence and, as with Jack and Lois, realize what magnificent spirits they possessed. I feel blessed and humbled to have been taken into their confidence and called friend. They became a part of my story and in the process, my being.

What a pair they were. They were such good solid people who managed to keep a twinkle in their eyes even after life threw them some knee-buckling blows.

Lois was a petite woman with short dark hair who loved the western novels of Louis L'Amour. This is of note because she had the grit and strong will of the female characters she adored. Her unconventional childhood – traveling to airshows in South Dakota and Montana with her father who performed as a barnstorming pilot – may have been the preparation she needed for the unconventional life that was to follow. She spoke with a distinctly sweet high-pitched voice, and from her stature and tone one might assume her fragile. Lois was anything but…

It was a long journey before she and Jack settled into Indian Creek. But soon after they did, Lois began collecting a menagerie of pets. And over the course of the years, Lois had a lot of pets. She had a duck named Sadie who would sit on her kitchen window sill and talk away to her for hours on end. During that same period Lois and Jack had a peacock and a number of ducks and geese, all of whom became dinner for the neighborhood coyotes, bobcats and mountain lions. By the time we met Jack and Lois, they had accumulated nine horses, one mule, two cats and three dogs, all of which fared better than their feathered friends.

Her two small dogs had an array of endearing (some might say, annoying) traits which Lois seemed to accentuate during their interactions. Mickey, her small rounded (toy) poodle never acted poodle-like. Maybe he didn't know! Lois would show Mickey off after his return from a groomer saying, "Marcie, look at Mickey; doesn't he look handsome?" Of course I would respond appropriately when, in reality, he looked anything but - with bows in his hair, nails painted and enough perfume to gag a roomful of people. After a bit Lois would say, "Oh Mickey, do you want to go outside?" Twenty minutes later, Mickey would return after having had a grand time r-o-l-l-i-n-g in the manure. Lois would invite him to jump on her lap and, waving her hand madly to disperse the odor say, "OH MICKEY, WHAT have you done?" That was it! That was his scolding! And there he would sit quite happy with himself, his bows in disarray and the odor of manure overtaking the room. The scenario was repeated every time Mickey visited the groomer!

Then there was Fang, a 107 year-old Chihuahua with no teeth and horrendous breath! The whole time we lived there, Fang was 107 years old. Lois kept saying, "Marcie, do you know that Fang is 107. Years. Old?" punctuating each word. She'd say, "Fang, come on honey, come sit on my lap." And Fang would jump up, panting with joy, while spewing his nasty breath! Lois would go, "OH FANG!", and turn her head away waving her hand by way of protection. Many a time I would come in their house and ask where Fang was and Lois would answer with her sweet voice, "In the dungeon." And leave it at that! It was not until later that I finally figured out that the dungeon was their closet. I'm afraid that Fang was relegated to the *dungeon* when guests were at hand.

Jack was tall and rangy without an ounce of fat on him – jean and boot clad, with a beat-up straw cowboy hat (felt, when the occasion called for it) – reminding me of John Wayne in the cadence of his speech. He had a relaxed drawl, was well-read on regional history, especially concerning Lewis and Clark's journey with their guide, Sacajawea, through the Lemhi Valley and Salmon River corridor regions in Idaho. He was self-taught at most anything one could name – mechanics, carpentry, horses, hunting. If he didn't know how to do something, he studied on it and asked questions. With his droll sense of humor, he easily picked up on human foibles so much on display in the outlying regions of North Fork and, by way of extension, developed into a mesmerizing storyteller.

As a teenager attending high school in Pocatello, Lois was courted by Jack and his brother, and she had great fun deciding who would capture her heart. Ultimately it had to be Jack; he was the most fun. She loved to tell the story of Jack picking her up for the prom in a 1940's car of some kind – one that he had fixed up. Lois was in a fluffy white gown and not wearing a coat. She mentioned that she was cold and Jack said, "Oh I'll fix that." He opened some kind of vent that allowed heat from the engine to gravitate to the car's cabin. (At least that was the idea.) Within moments they were both covered by a thick cloud of black substance! The night was ruined – her dress was ruined! Completely flustered, mouth agape, she looked over at Jack, only to see him completely covered in soot himself with a slight grin etching itself on his face, and the merest shrug of the shoulders. Laugh or cry? They chose to laugh and couldn't stop. Lois was in love. It was going to be one adventure after another.

Shortly after graduation Jack and Lois married and eventually had a sweet daughter named Theresa. After Lois's graduation from nursing school, they purchased land in the hills of Pocatello in order to build a house. However, fate threw a wrench in those plans – Jack was struck with tetanus which resulted in lock-jaw. He was hospitalized in critical condition, and Lois was told that he might not make it through the night. He made it, but not without side effects.

Jack was left with debilitating migraines and frayed nerves, sometimes throwing him into dark mood swings. The once light-hearted, easy-going Jack had disappeared, at times shunning family and friends alike.

Lois was not to be daunted; they had purchased the property in order to build a house, and build a house they would. Although Jack did not want to have anything to do with the idea, it didn't faze Lois. She decided that she and her father would start the project with or without Jack's assistance! She knew that they could not afford to pay rent while building, so the two of them pitched a wall tent for the entire family to live in on the edge of their property. Gradually, ever so gradually, Jack began to join in. It took about a year and a half, but when they were done, they had a lovely new home and Jack assumed he was in for a nice respite. His dark moods were becoming less frequent as were his battles with migraines. His once easy-going personality was returning.

What Jack did not realize was that Lois was contemplating something that would have far- reaching effects on their lives, not to mention the complete healing of Jack. Lois decided that she wanted a horse. She matter-of-factly told her husband this and said that she had one picked out. Naturally Jack was dumbfounded, given that Lois didn't know the first thing about horses! Lois said that she would learn. Jack stated that he didn't want to have anything to do with this; she was on her own! Yet before Lois could even contemplate her next step, she saw Jack out there building a corral, installing a water trough and shelter.

Lois didn't say anything. When the day came for Lois to get her horse and ride it home Jack said, "Lois I don't think you should be the one to do that. It's too dangerous for you to be riding a horse up this winding mountain road. I'll ride it for you." Late that afternoon Jack rode up on a beautiful palomino named Lady. Well, before Lois knew it, Jack was out there feeding and brushing and working with Lady. She became Jack's horse! What could Lois do but get herself another horse – a spirited chestnut with four white socks and star on her forehead. Lois named her Gypsy; the proud pair were made for each other.

While in Pocatello Jack was fleet and maintenance manager for the family laundry business and Lois was a nurse at the Pocatello General Hospital. When Theresa was eleven, they moved to Salmon to take over a family member's failing laundry business. This move only added to their repertoire of delightful tales and some which tugged at the heart. One such was when Jack and a female friend of theirs, a bubbly extrovert (I'll call her Marge because I've forgotten her name), decided to test the rapidity of the gossip-train in Salmon. So Marge climbed in the truck with Jack, comfortably tucking herself under his arm, and they drove right through the main drag, radio blasting, laughing and carrying on. Within five minutes Lois's phone was ringing off the hook!! Lois kept responding, "Reeeally?" But of course the joke was on the town and the phone exchange operators passing on the myriad of can't-wait-to-share messages, not Lois.

Another time they were up in Challis at a bar for some event, and this rather drunk man who was sitting next to Lois kept bugging her to dance. Lois finally told him in no uncertain terms that if he didn't leave her alone, he was going to have to deal with her husband who was very jealous. Undaunted, he kept after her. Finally, Lois tapped Jack on the shoulder and said, "Jack, Jack, this man is bothering me; would you make him stop?" Jack turned around and said, "Lois, what is it?! I'm trying to talk here!!!" Well the drunk loved that!! He said, "Ha! Jealous, huh? Come on lady, let's dance!"

During Lois's work days at the laundry, she would take out the trash to the back alley. More times than not, she would find a young boy there by the name of Tom. Each time he would say, "If I were your son, I would take out the trash for you." Lois was always touched by him but didn't know what to make of it. Eventually Jack and Lois purchased a 160-acre ranch down the Salmon River from North Fork. They kept the laundry business while they labored long hours rehabbing and moving broken down cabins, repairing fences and purchasing horses (some of which were saved from the glue factory) in order to turn the property into a dude ranch, ultimately naming it Indian Creek Guest Ranch.

One day they received a call from a judge in Salmon saying that he had a boy in his chambers who wanted them to be his parents. It was nine-year-old Tom. Apparently Tom's mother was drunk most of the time and had totally neglected him. He never knew his father. After the initial shock Jack and Lois said, of course, yes, they would adopt Tom. And from that moment on they poured their love into him. His teeth had numerous cavities on top of an array of health issues to resolve, but Lois, being the loving and capable nurse she was, was the perfect mother for him.

I don't know how long – months, years – this took, but eventually Tom was their son. However, before that could legally take place, it was necessary for Lois to appear in court with Tom in Idaho Falls. The landscape between Salmon and Idaho Falls has the feel of a moonscape – flat, arid, high lonesome, with mountains and sparsely spaced ranches seeming to float in the distance as mirages. Rarely, and especially back then, did one see movement other than the occasional jack rabbit or tumbleweed, especially not from another car on this highway. It was somewhere in this between area that Lois's car was hit broadside by a car going ninety miles an hour at a crossing. If it had not been for the older Cadillac she and Tom were in, they would have been killed. As it was, Lois sustained massive head injuries, leaving her with blood spurting from her skull. Remarkably, a friend of hers was in a car behind them. I can't imagine how the man managed to bandage her head and get her to an Idaho Falls hospital. The brain surgeon was just leaving for vacation when she was rushed in. Although after the surgery Lois was in a coma, she could hear people talking about her saying things like, "Poor dear," and, "I wonder if she'll ever be able to walk again." Lois said that she wondered who they were talking about. She had no idea that they were referring to her. When she eventually woke up, she was blind and unable to walk!

I keep thinking of poor young Tom during this time, trying initially to answer questions regarding his relationship to Lois and not knowing if he were about to lose his new mom. That must have been such a traumatic event for him to experience at such a young age.

Eventually Lois's sight did return and she was able to walk with the use of a cane. She said that one day she walked out of one of the cabins at the ranch and called to Jack. He looked up to see her tossing the cane out of reach as she walked in a wobbly fashion across the yard!! She never picked up a cane again. Her recovery might seem miraculous, and maybe some of it was, but my guess is that it was Lois's sheer determination which brought her back from seemingly insurmountable physical injuries. Pain, however, accompanied her the rest of her life, but I'll be darned if she would let anyone know it! Only those who knew her intimately might perceive a slight limp, while she held her head up high as if all was normal. In order to get her through the rehabilitation process, she had taken constant doses of aspirin, not knowing at the time that it could and would cause kidney damage. The whole time I knew Lois, she had bouts with kidney infections and would be in excruciating pain – sometimes bedridden. Yet she would put on a brave face for her guests as she and Jack beguiled them with fun stories of life on the ranch and living in the mountains. Lois would have to take an antibiotic containing sulfa to fight each infection and that made her sick to her stomach. During those times when we were invited to eat dinner with the guests, I could tell by the pasty look on her face when an infection was at hand. At some point during dinner she would get up, retreat to the bathroom, throw up and return as if nothing was wrong.

Lois was an amazing woman whom I came to love and admire deeply. Anytime I was going through a rough patch she would simply say, "Keep your chin up Marcie." And knowing the life's trials from which that advice came, I took it to heart then as I continue to do now.

We came to Idaho for our honeymoon in the early '80's. We took a three day raft trip down the Salmon River, experiencing heart pounding wild rapids as well as calm views of mountain goats and big horn sheep looking benignly down upon us from their rocky perches. And the campouts under a million-zillion stars took one's breath away.

After that we came to stay at the Indian Creek Guest Ranch for five days, not realizing that it would change the trajectory of our lives. The ranch's lower gate was about one-tenth of a mile up the canyon from Indianola, the Salmon National Forest's helicopter station. Indian Creek flowed into the Salmon River with the canyon itself exiting onto the Salmon River Road. The Salmon River Road followed the course of the river for a thirty-mile stretch, the territory becoming more primitive and sparsely populated with each mile, eventually coming to an end as the river flowed onward eventually joining with the Snake River. As soon as we passed through the first gate and began the slow three mile trek up the rock strewn ranch road, we felt like we had arrived in an oasis. Not a spa-like oasis – no, this was too cut off from the outside world – too basic for anything like that. The road, bordered on the left by emerald green pastures fed by cool water spilling over irrigation ditches, was starkly set against a backdrop of arid mountain foothills on either side. The grazing horses barely noticed as we passed by. Soft-needled ponderosa pine trees followed the road's edge all the way to the top gate. It was one of those moments where one needs to pinch oneself to make sure the experience is real: magical is the only word which comes to mind. Yes, we felt we had entered a magical place – a retreat from the harsh environment outside its gates. After the fun but tiring float trip, we felt the ranch wrap its arms around us.

When we arrived at the main ranch house we were immediately enchanted with the laid back atmosphere, staying in one of their several guest log cabins. After an initial day of becoming familiar with our surroundings, feeding the horses, chopping wood, hiking up the nearest hill and sitting around a campfire at night, we were ready to branch out. Jack rode horses with us up to the former Ulysses and Kitty Burton Gold Mines, stopping on the way to show us a little red cabin bejeweled by sunlight. Once at Ulysses it was fascinating poking our heads in abandoned log cabins, mine buildings, stables and even a blacksmith shop – all tucked in scattered areas along the canyon walls. We learned of one miner who, having lived across the Salmon River at the base of the canyon, would hike 9 miles to work every day. Amazing... Some of the exterior wood found on the mine buildings had weathered richly golden, streaked with black. Another day Lois made us a picnic lunch and Jack drove us in his truck following the backroads of their canyon up to Indian Peak cresting at 7,700 ft. One could see in the hazy distance for miles – a perfect spot to enjoy a picnic and feel at perfect peace.

The day before our arrival, unbeknownst to us, Tom, their son, had visited them and told them that he had decided on a career in law enforcement. Jack and Lois felt that he had seemed relieved and happy with his decision. Little did they know that that would be the last time they would see him. He told them that he was headed to Boise the next day and would call them when he got there. They never received that call. Jack and Lois had put on such a brave front to us, we would never have known what was going on unless their friends, Bud and Dorothy, had not pulled us aside and said that Tom was missing. The day before we left, Bud and Dorothy told us that Tom had been found in his truck just over Lost Trail Pass in Montana, dead, with a gunshot to his head. His rifle was on the seat beside him. It was ruled a suicide. I wrote a long note to them and left it in our room expressing our heartfelt sympathies. Apparently there is no place on earth, even an idyllic place such as this, where tragedy cannot strike.

After our return to Kansas City, Lois and I began communicating by letter, sharing recipes and news. Eventually, I learned the little red cabin we had briefly viewed on our way to Ulysses was for rent. And, without much discussion, Bernie and I decided to throw caution to the wind, give up perfectly good careers, and move there. I have come to believe that we were the right people to be in close proximity to Jack and Lois during their time of grieving. Because everything was new to us and we had not known Tom, they were able to relive their memories of him by sharing stories with us, and found in those stories was a celebration of Tom's life. I know that I was of particular comfort to Lois as she kept asking, "Why?" No answers were ever known for sure, but at least Lois was able to voice the questions privately to me. And Jack was able to distract himself by teaching Bernie the ways of the West – like felling trees and bringing in firewood and posthole digging in rock strewn country, and "irritating" (irrigating). It is my hope that our presence up that isolated canyon brought some comfort to them during those initial years of mourning their much-loved son.

As happens with much of life's experiences, we are unaware of the lessons gained while living through them. That was certainly true of my time with Jack and Lois. Viewed from the outside one might think of their lives as depressing or tragic in a way – given their hardships. The opposite is true; they were the most resilient people I have ever known. At every turn, they chose Life – to go forward and live life in all its fullness. And they did so with grit and generosity and humor. They kept their chins up.

Jack & Lois & Nappy

Lois, Jack, Theresa, and dogs Mickey & Nappy

Jack & his new pup, Buckles

Indian Creek Ranch

DIAMONDBACK

With the snow receding from the high country, the first hints of spring's awakening come to Indian Creek canyon could be found in the trees stretching their skeletal tips skyward, rewarding those below with the first sight of long-hoped-for tender buds. It was an achingly slow process I would come to discover, with the sun's rays grudgingly sharing their warmth in this particularly tight part of the canyon.

The days had been soakingly dreary for the two months we had lived here, not affording many opportunities to hike and explore much beyond the confines of our front door. I knew I needed to establish familiar haunts if I were ever to find comfort in this our new home – our own cabin in the woods. The setting was storybook enough – situated about a mile up the road from the guest ranch, it sat on the far side of the creek on a rise above a hand hewn footbridge. The cabin's faded red logs framed in white by its windows and doors sat comfortably tucked against the ridge to its back, seemingly making a last stand against the encroaching forest as it nestled down into the earth. At the cabin's front, Indian Creek tumbled its way toward the Salmon River. Lining the creek's banks, an established thicket of raspberry bushes asserted their dominion over all except for a stone patio and fire pit sitting in their midst just above water level. Surrounding the cabin on three sides was a lush green lawn. And during the tight time-frame when the sun struck, the property lit up like an earth-encrusted emerald washed clean by rain. At those times, the cabin, poor as it was, seemed to speak to chasers of dreams on a visceral level.

No denying it – picturesque, yes – but there were bears out there, somewhere…coming out of hibernation, they'd be eating their way down the canyon, and with little ones in tow! Great…I peeked through the front door pane, turned the knob and stepped out. The sun had edged its way over the tree tops and held some warmth. If I could make it to the north pasture, the last leg before the ranch house – that would be a very good thing. Our newly-acquired husky mix, Timber, and Lady, eagerly sat at attention anticipating their first adventure. *Let's go!* And they were off.

Crossing the red footbridge, I swung open the hand-forged iron gate, ringing its cowbell in the process, as the dogs scrambled past my legs and burst onto the canyon road. *Freedom!!!* Up and down the timbered hills they ran, unfocused and half-crazed with pent up energy. Every few minutes one or the other or both would cross in front of me, weaving their way through the brush toward nothing in particular.

Even though it was 10:00 in the morning and our cabin was soaking up the sun's rays, the shadowed part of the canyon road I was hiking still held a chill. As we neared the last bend before the upper pasture, the road flattened and the trees gave way to a small grassy opening, and I spotted a smooth stone ledged above the creek from which to dangle my feet and bask in the sun. So soothing, so safe, the cadence of the stream carrying me away while Lady, off on some chase, left Timber to prance at the water's edge, drink, explore and become hot – deciding to visit me with wagging tail, panting mouth and dripping body.

Drowsy and slow to react, I heard, "C-h-h-h-i-i-i-i," and looked down between my legs – freezing. Large, distinct diamond patterns on brown scaly skin accompanied by, "C-h-h-h-i-i-i-i." *No-o-o...,* the dreaded rattlesnake, the stuff of death in Westerns! And me, with my two dogs, up Indian Creek, with my bear bells on! Big help. Timber had alerted the snake to his existence, but apparently not to mine. The inches between its head and my legs seemed reduced to millimeters the longer Timber stood by my side panting, dripping, wagging – completely oblivious to the ever-so-focused presence of peril at my feet. Then, as if a crescendo had been reached, Timber peeled off to indulge once more in play at water's edge. The rattlesnake relaxed, slipped silently into the brush, taking with it the bit of peace I had claimed.

I sat for a moment, inhaling the mountain air, fragrant with the wild flowers of the day, then stood, a little wiser, contemplating the juxtaposition of beauty (even the exquisitely engineered rattlesnake) and danger and the safety net of instincts and called Timber and Lady for our stroll back up the canyon.

Me with Timber & Lady

JOHN'S CABIN

The name "John's cabin" was given to it by Jack and Lois in memory of their friend, John, who lived there five or so months a year until his passing. According to them, he was a "tough ole Swede" whom they loved as much for the entertainment of his temperament as for his loyalty to them. It was leased to us by his son, Martin, who lived in Boise, Idaho at the time. The lease involved fairly reasonable terms on the condition that we allowed him and a friend or two to stay with us a couple of times a year during steelhead season.

The red L-shaped log cabin sat on a rise above the tumbling waters of Indian Creek looking out over the creek onto a deeply-shaded red barn which sat on the far side of the road. With the creek at its front and a timbered canyon wall to its back, the cabin was carpeted on either side by a lush green lawn gently sloping along with the fall of the creek. Sprinklers tapped into spring water that had been channeled by way of a ditch on the uphill side of the lawn.

The ditch was straddled by a small red wooden structure with a pitched roof that held tin cups, whereby one could get a cool drink on a warm day. Running the length of the irrigation ditch was a 2 foot wide strawberry patch, and on the ditch's far side immediately before its waters dropped off into the creek was a nice patch of rhubarb. The original 15 foot raised footbridge spanning Indian Creek had chest high handrails on either side and, as you might imagine, was painted red. As a person stepped onto the bridge, there was a white hand-forged iron gate from which hung a cow bell, quite adequately announcing any arrival.

The cabin had three doors, one at the back basically allowing direct entrance into a mine shaft if one so desired (which I didn't), and the other two entered the kitchen, one at the front and the other, a Dutch door, on the north or high side of the yard. The front porch entrance was softened on one side of the concrete pad by wild Columbine and on the other side by a large Service Berry bush, both of which bloomed in the spring. The front door and the inside doorway at the far end of the kitchen leading into the living/bedroom portion basically ensured a pathway which divided the room in half, with essentials to either side. To the right, just inside the front door, was a full cabinet with a small work surface. It faced the side of two stoves – the first was propane and beside it was a wood cooking stove. The only problem with the second is that the oven couldn't be used for cooking because of an inner cracked plate. It was primarily used to heat the kitchen when needed. On the far side of the Dutch door and facing the two stoves and cabinet was a large porcelain kitchen sink with cold spring water available to one of the two faucets. The hot water line had not been hooked up and, surprise, the only person small enough to fit in the crawl space to run that line was me! *Nope. I didn't sign up for that! I'd rather haul water from the bathroom thank you.* On the left side of the room as one entered was an antique Hoosier cabinet that we brought with us, thank heavens, as it gave me another work surface. In the center between that and the small propane refrigerator was our large round oak dining table. A propane chandelier light hung in the center of the room.

There was a propane heater readily available in the living/bedroom to provide adequate heat. And if we had so chosen, we could have used it. However, given the price of propane, we chose to install a wood heating stove and provide our own wood for the winter months. The bathroom at the far end of the main living area did not have a heat source. Light was provided by wall-mounted propane light fixtures which we supplemented with oil-burning tabletop antique lamps.

To our utter surprise and horror we discovered after our arrival that the source of water for the cabin came from a spring source 1,100 feet up the mountain on the opposite side of the road. The flexible water line ran down the mountain, under the road, through the creek and then rested on top of our lawn until it entered the cabin. The horror of it was that we had a water bed with no electric source to heat it! Our joints ached for a good two weeks until the water in the bed began to reach room temperature!! During that time we slept on top of the blankets!!!

The barn housed our generator, and during that first summer, I put it to good use given that I was determined to keep our clothes ironed. I would haul out the sprinkled clothes in the laundry basket, along with my iron and ironing board, to a parking space just outside the barn. Then I would fire up the generator and iron. It was so funny to see the double takes of those few passersby as I stood in the great outdoors, ironing away!! Eventually, as Lois promised, I soon quit bothering with it; nobody ironed their clothes out there. I will admit though on occasion – special occasions – I heated the antique iron on my propane stove and ironed those clothes deemed necessary, scorching a few in the process. Old habits die hard.

During that first summer we had planted a vegetable garden on the far side of the irrigation ditch. It was maddening – I kept finding our tender sprouts having been trampled by some hooved animal with monster-sized feet. We thought maybe it was an elk. That was until the day I looked out the front door, only to be greeted by a magnificent young bull moose with rich brown and black coloring sporting an impressive rack, standing about 15 feet away!!! At the sight of me, he turned and I can describe it no other way, glided through the creek, across the road and disappeared into the forest, leaving me breathless. I've never witnessed another animal move with such ease and grace before or since. And to add to the wonder of it, Jack said that it was quite rare to find a moose in our area. In fact I never saw another one. After that I forgave any damage done to our garden. I thought – *have at it you rare and beautiful beast!*

I was hired by the U. S. Forest Service during our first summer in Idaho and we had made it through our first winter in the mountains, having been laid off in late fall. The snow pack at higher elevations was tremendous that winter and initially had thawed at a slow rate. However, temperatures that second spring warmed quickly, and the creeks and rivers filled rapidly and soon became torrents of raging, frothing muddy water. It was still dark as we were leaving our cabin one morning to join the planting crews. I came out first and saw that our foot bridge had been pushed by a log jam onto its side, leaving it at a 30 degree angle!! I said, "Bernie, the bridge is gone!! Well, it's not gone but, but, it's, it's…" I didn't need to finish – he came running out. That bridge was our only means of egress to the road! Bernie told me to cross the bridge and go to work!!! You have to trust someone with your life to follow those directions! I did as told, hanging on for dear life to the upper handrail to keep myself from being washed away by the roiling creek. When I came home that evening, Bernie had righted the bridge. He had chained the support poles on either end to tree trunks and then used a chainsaw to cut through the two center supports, thus allowing them and the log jam to break free. Prior to the flood, Bernie, with the help of his son Mat who had come to live with us, had just replaced the former red bridge with this new one. Jack had advised not to put in the center supports, fearing this exact outcome. Lesson learned.

There was always something in need of doing. Between felling trees, cutting them up and hauling them home to supply 10 cords of wood for the winter months and fall hunting in hopes of bringing in two deer and one elk for our meat supply, we kept busy. Also, while Bernie was splitting wood, I was cooking large quantities of food to provide 'instant' meals during the work season. Plus we so enjoyed having friends to dinner. I would cook all day, making pies and bread and the main dish. It's during those visits one expected tall tales to be told. The more the details were embellished, the better. On occasion we'd even drive over Lost Trail Pass into Montana just to go to dinner with Jack and Lois. That was considered a big night out!

Plus, you just never knew what was going to happen. I can't quite put my finger on why this was. Maybe it was living away from civilization as we knew it. At times I felt like I was living on a different planet – the world outside our bubble seemed intent on busying itself with each new technological invention (to make life easier), and it had nothing to do with us. When in the early 1980's your means of communication with the outside world was via a crank phone system or a pay phone, you were basically living in a different universe. In fact, a small gas station about five miles downriver from us called the Shoup Store still had gas pumps in which one had to crank the gas into the pump's upper chamber before it could flow into the car's tank!!

It might put things in perspective to end with how a particular couple in Salmon viewed the state of our cabin. They were owners of one of the local grocery stores in town. They took a liking to us and invited us to dinner along with another couple at their home which was situated in a subdivision humorously termed by locals as "Snob Hill."

We had enjoyed a lovely meal and the evening was winding down when the hostess asked where exactly we lived up Indian Creek. They knew we were neighbors of Jack and Lois, and apparently that held some cachet with them. When I shared that we lived in the little red cabin a mile up the canyon from the Indian Creek Ranch, the woman exclaimed, "Oh, no, you couldn't possibly live there!! Why that is nothing but a shack!!" When I answered in the affirmative that, yes, we were speaking of the same cabin, she only became more exasperated. Yep, that's exactly how it played out. And so ended any further desire on our part to grocery shop at their store!

John's cabin in winter's blanket

Bernie & Mat on the bridge they had just built

Barn across the creek from the cabin

U.S. FOREST SERVICE SEASONAL WORK

Working as a seasonal employee for the U.S. Forest Service opened up a whole new world to me. As with most opportunities, it ended up blessing my life by means unimaginable to a young woman from the Midwest. It introduced me to talented strong women of the same ilk as me in that they possessed a basic love of and respect for nature and the outdoors. I was assigned to a variety of crews during my three seasons with the Forest Service, mostly populated by women. Each position required strong physical stamina, while imposing an unwritten code among the crews of enduring whatever discomforts one might be feeling physically. To be teamed with a complainer was a real downer; the semi-arid mountainous terrain and elements were demanding enough in and of themselves. We were there for each other, and no whining please.

After 'surviving' my first gloomy and somewhat isolated spring in the mountains, I was elated when hired in late spring by the Salmon Ranger District to assist the Silviculturist (Forester), Doug Basford, in collecting information from selected tree species for a timber management research project he was conducting. With clipboard in hand, I basically served as a record keeper of the information he fed me as we drove over a dizzying array of roads, stopping at specified stands in order to hike through the forest until we came upon each tree he was looking for. It was interesting work and gave me an overview of the managed forests within our scope. After completion of that project, I was assigned for the summer to mark trees for the thinning crews.

To put it simply, we were to mark trees to be left standing by Forest Service sawyer crews. In other words, trees were thinned out in order to accelerate the growth of those remaining. My working partner was an unassuming woman by the name of Maria, who in time became a dear and treasured friend. At first meeting, she greeted me with a soft hello from behind a pair of oval glasses. Her long coal black hair was held off her face by means of a ponytail at the nape of her neck. She wore a featureless light blue cotton blouse, khaki slacks and heavy-duty hiking boots which had been greased for water repellency. She stood 4' 11" tall. (When asked she would reply that she was almost 5 feet.) She wore no makeup to enhance her deep olive skin. She was the first person I had ever met that lived without pretense.

It was a shadowless dreary day, causing the mountainous terrain to be virtually void of feature as we drove to our assigned stand of timber. After arriving at the designated unit, we each had a cup of hot tea from our thermoses and chatted a bit. After exiting the truck, Maria loaded my backpack with extra cans of spray paint (sky blue) used to mark trees and then walked along the road with me, indicating the orange flags running up either side of the slope and shared that those were the borders of our unit. She then gave me a brief lesson on marking the trees for thinning. The priority species, Douglas fir, was to remain standing. We then were to prioritize the other species leaving those which had minimum trunk diameters of 8 inches and space the remaining trees fifteen feet apart. Also, Maria explained the necessity of leaving snag trees as well as bushy boggy areas for wildlife. We then climbed the cut-bank, found our meeting point halfway between the two flagged boundaries, and each began working alone.

Initially I found myself in the middle of a thicket of small Douglas fir. I became so turned around that I wasn't quite sure what I had marked. After a while I found myself getting into a rhythm and could remember the trees behind me. I would simply work my way across the slope, parallel to the road, moving from the outside flagged border to the middle of the unit and back again to the border and so on as I gradually progressed up the mountain side. I would know I was in the middle of the unit when I came upon Maria's paint marks. I found it to be relaxing work, but on this first day, a bit lonesome. Grey was all around; I could see no further than 30 feet in any direction. There was no indication that anyone else was about except for the occasional blue marks left on the bordering trees by Maria.

Silence seemed unbounded and unfortunately as was the capacity of my imagination. *Is this it? Is this what it is going to be like? I'll shrivel up from loneliness. Am I doing this right? My work is now for the world to see – everyone will know if I've done it wrong! Where is Maria?* And so on…

Just when my mind was beginning to run amuck I heard the soft voice of Maria, "How are you doing?"

"Oh, okay. I'm not quite sure I marked these correctly though."

"Let me take a look." And she did. "They look okay. You're getting the hang of it. Do you want to take a break?"

"YES!"

Together we sat on the damp ground and leaned against a log. Her quiet soul began to talk of marking trees, of this region, of her life – coming from a large family in Mexico, marrying the local high school English teacher – and then I spoke of mine. And so began a ritual which became a hallmark of our friendship. I told her about my grandmother from Australia who said that everyone has a bundle to carry through life – sometimes it is quite heavy and at other times, light. The important thing, though, was that each of us must carry our own bundle. Many times upon our breaks we would ask about each other's bundles. Being able to share a heavy load or something light and fun in this way was such a sacred way for me to honor my beloved Grandmother Elsie.

The next spring, along with another woman (her name escapes me), I was sent to Boise for a course on becoming a tree planting inspector. Each spring, reforestation crews fan out over clear-cut mountain slopes to plant approximately 125,000 two-year old tree seedlings on nine-foot grids. It is a fairly straight-forward process. The first crews to hit the slopes were known as scalpers. It was each person's task on this crew to scrape a two-foot square area, freeing it of grass and weeds. This crew was followed by men or women wielding heavy gasoline powered augers who would drill a hole in the center of each scalped area. The third crew consisted of the actual tree planters. They carried seedlings in small burlap sacks attached to their waists and mostly worked on their hands and knees, planting the trees in the newly-created holes. Along with the other inspector, my job was to come along behind the tree planters and dig up a prescribed number of seedlings per grid layout in order to inspect for proper planting techniques, those techniques being to plant each tree in the center of the prescribed hole, leaving the roots to spread out with the main stem left upright. Those plantings which failed the tests fell into three basic categories, each of which would cause the tree to die in the long run. The crews thus earned nicks to their records for: first, if someone had placed the roots against the side of a hole, rather than the middle, thus not allowing the roots enough loose soil to spread out; second, if they had planted it so deep that it would cause the end of the root to touch the bottom of the hole, thus forcing the root back into a "J" formation, causing those roots to ultimately strangle themselves; and third, planting the neck of the stem below the soil grade, eventually smothering the tree. Let it be known that except for inspecting, this was cold, tiring, difficult, muddy work. Everyone wore tough chaps either to protect their legs from the equipment they were using or to keep the mud from becoming caked on their clothes. Thus while inspecting the work was less taxing, we did not find ourselves in a popular position at camp each night. Each crew chief was pushing their crews to plant the most with the least amount of errors and with each error sighted, we were definitely standing in the way of those goals. However, given that the survival rate for this area's reforestation efforts was only 10% at best, I knew the value of our quality control work and was therefore comfortable in my role.

After the tree planting season came to a close, I took a course provided locally by the Salmon Ranger District to learn the skills required to be on the Stand Exam Crew. At the end of the classroom course we were given a timed field test to see if we had the wherewithal to measure up. That test was intense to say the least! However, I PASSED! I was very proud and excited. I was teamed with Tawna, our crew leader. Tawna also became and remains a good and valued friend. I loved working on this crew. Our task was to hike into unlogged areas and record information that would be used to make timber stand management decisions. In each drainage we were sent to, we would be given aerial photos and topography maps delineating various acreages of timber stands, called units. Usually those boundaries were determined by ridge tops, drainages, tree species, rock slides, etc. The number of plots we threw was directly determined by the acreage at hand. The plots were 30 feet in diameter and within that field we recorded the tree species, their diameters, crown ratios and densities. Every so often we hand drilled into a tree, taking a core sample in order to count the rings, thus determining the tree's age. Records were noted of the habitat contained within each thirty foot plot. This included ground covers and bushes, the pitch of the slope etc. This helped our silviculturist in determining the overall moisture retention of the site.

Many times on the way to the assigned timber stands, we had to cross a rancher's land, and it became a game as to who could successfully 'unlock' the convoluted wire gate closures each rancher used. There was a definite method to their madness and it was to keep interlopers out. Not only did we have to undo the wire 'locks', we had to put them back the way we found them!! Some of us were better than others, but we enjoyed the challenge even though we moaned when it was our turn.

After arriving at a site and before collecting our gear, we literally mapped out our day. The job of using the compass and finding the center of each plot was rotated every other day between partners. After mapping out the plots in the unit, three additional things had to be determined before a crew could begin their hike: 1) Determine the distance to the center of the first plot and then from center to center between all subsequent plots; 2) set the compass reading correctly; and, 3) determine the number of paces between each plot. A couple of points of note: 1) Obviously this was before GPS; and, 2) every crew member knew the number of paces it took them to walk (pace) on flat land 20 ft. So that was figured into the equation when determining the number of paces needed from point to point. The tricky part was adjusting our pace counting according to the degree of slope, as we climbed over logs, around obstructions, over rock slides, through creek beds etc. And if we were off either in using our compass (possibly by tilting it slightly) or in our pacing count, we would not end up back at our truck at the end of the day. That never happened. We were always, always, right.

I remember one particularly difficult unit to traverse because of its undulating ground and horde of biting insects wherein Tawna's notes read, "This unit is only fit for the wildlife and the mosquitos that guard it so fiercely." Exactly.

One fall we were traversing terrain with a good 10" of snow on the ground. We kept cutting the tracks of a mountain lion. It was a bit unsettling because it was quite obvious that the animal was circling us. And even more unsettling when we returned to our truck to find that it had even checked out our trucks. If not for the snow on the ground, we would have been totally oblivious to the danger.

Another time, also in late fall, our crews were camped out up Moose Creek drainage which bordered a designated Wilderness Area. Tawna and I had put in a long day yet could tell from our topography map that there was a tall cliff overlooking the Wilderness Area just beyond where we stood. Tired as we were, we decided we had to take a quick look. Oh my... First, as we were hiking up the treeless incline to the cliff's edge, at the point where the cliff jutted out, 30 feet from us a magnificent buck with a full rack abruptly stood up, looked straight at us for a long moment, and then bounded off in all of his breathtaking glory. We had been oblivious to his existence until that moment – it was heart stopping. To our right bordering the open area we were traversing was a dense stand of timber. As we moved forward, paralleling it, without warning a thunderous roar came from the timber; then, total silence coupled with the overpowering smell of elk urine. A large herd of elk (maybe 50+) had been bedded down and our presence obviously unnerved them. All we saw was a wall of elk hind quarters as they exited. Tawna and I were breathless by that point. After we calmed ourselves, we hiked to the edge of the cliff and lay on our stomachs overlooking the Wilderness Area. To our utter amazement, we counted upwards of 100 elk! We gave that count to our most appreciative Fish & Game Warden, Russ Kozacek. What a day for us! Those moments of sheer wonder remain crystallized in my mind. They were pure gifts.

Tree planting crew - that's me 3rd from right

Tree planting crew - that's me top row second from left

From left to right, me, Megan, & Tawna (Stand Exam Crew)

That's me in front of my Forest Service tent

Chatting with Maria, a potter as well as Forest Service worker

Here I am standing in front of a Ponderosa Pine

WINTERS

What did we do for entertainment during the long winter months? Well, there was always firewood to split. We needed 10 cords a winter – that's a lot of felling of trees, hauling and wood splitting. You deal with it by getting into the Zen of it – focusing on the fragrance of the pitch, the feel of the axe in your hand, and the crack of the wood when it splits in two. And in so doing, a natural flow and rhythm develops in your movements. It becomes a peaceful task rather than an arduous one. Other than that, we played a lot of UNO, and on Sunday nights listened to radio broadcasts of "Fibber McGee and Mollie" and "The Shadow." We both enjoyed reading passages from *All Creatures Great and Small,* a book filled with humorous and heartwarming true life stories of a young veterinarian's experiences in rural Yorkshire, England in the late 1930's. If I were alone, I listened to the radio during the day. We primarily received two stations – one was the local station out of Salmon and the other, strangely enough, was from Los Angeles! (It was surreal to listen to traffic reports from

L.A. while living in a remote mountainous area.) At times the Salmon station was unintentionally funny. During a local swap- shop broadcast a caller kept saying she wanted to sell venison blinds. No matter how many times the host tried to correct her, indicating that she must mean venetian blinds, she was having none of it. During another of the call-in programs it was a particularly quiet day. The announcer kept saying, "Well, if anyone wants to call and say anything about anything, our lines are open!" Then long silences. Then he would repeat himself, "Well..." Finally someone called from a phone booth and said, "We were just passing through and heard your broadcast and decided that you needed HELP!" The announcer took great umbrage at this, "No. I don't!" This went back and forth, "Yes. You do!" Only in a small town... I loved it!

During each season except winter we received mail three days a week. It was delivered to our mail box at the base of Indian Creek Canyon by Wes Dorman, the owner of the Shoup Store, downriver from Indian Creek. Whether or not the Salmon River Road remained open to vehicle traffic in the winter very much depended on there being logging in the area. If not, it remained unplowed, that usually being the case. And unless the snowfall was exceptionally deep, Wes would then deliver the mail by snow machine. However, if avalanches blocked the road, he would resort to using skis. Given that skiing resulted in a three day trip for him, logic told us that our mail would be delivered once a week, at least until the snow slides cleared.

Winter was when I made my first fledgling attempt at cross-country skiing. My worthy instructor and good friend was Sue Kozacek. Sue was a Range Conservationist with the Bureau of Land Management (BLM). Her working closely with ranchers concerning grazing rights on government lands necessitated Sue having any range of skills including cross-country skiing and being a proficient horsewoman. So when I asked for a lesson, Sue took me to one of her pastures and patiently instructed me on the arm and leg rhythm necessary to successfully cross country ski. Although I couldn't seem to get the hang of it then I've become fairly accomplished at this late date. I have no doubt that Sue's long ago lessons finally kicked in.

In the winter we would snowmobile with neighbors Jack and Lois a lot, tracing the switchbacks up to the Indian Peak area. That area provided a wonderland with snow-packed meadows to play on and forests to create trails through. The first time we went up with them, I was in a full body snow suit. We stopped so I could relieve myself behind a tree. I had to pull down the whole outfit and too late I realized that I was peeing onto the inside of the snow suit!!!!! It was soaked!! I called to Bernie and he came over. I asked him, "What am I going to do?" His reply, "Wear. It." EVERYONE was laughing but me!! Wet pee all down my back!! It was awful!! I shudder even now just thinking about it. Admittedly I would have been laughing too if it hadn't involved me!!!

Another winter the snow was so deep that there were at least five avalanches covering the Salmon River Road between Indian Creek and North Fork. That road was perilous at best during the winter months because it was never plowed. Because of the snow's depth, the deer were finding it difficult to forage and consequently were starving. Russ Kozacek, our local Fish and Game Warden and Sue's husband at the time, contacted us via Jack and Lois and asked if Bernie would build twelve feed trays and place them up and down Indian Creek and other Salmon River corridor drainages. When they met up, Russ showed Bernie a map indicating where well-worn trails had been established by split-hooved animals over thousands of years. He said to place the trays beside those trails. After that at prearranged times Russ delivered sacks of food pellets and bails of alfalfa hay at the nearest avalanche to North Fork. Bernie used our snow machine with an attached sled that he had built to navigate over the slides in order to pick up the supplies. This was quite an operation and went on for weeks. The deer got so used to him coming that they would stand just to the side of the troughs when Bernie drove up. That trust is quite unusual.

Thank heavens Theresa had purposely left her car at North Fork before that particular winter set in. At those times when the isolation became unbearable, we placed our baskets full of laundry in the hand built sled and snowmobiled to North Fork, drove Theresa's car to Salmon, did our laundry, ate dinner and took in a movie. We then repeated our steps, ultimately heading back downriver, this time in the dark. During that winter cabin fever was a real thing for me, and the necessity of getting out of the canyon was worth every freezing minute on the snow machine.

Bernie's son, my step-son, Mat, lived with us from around age 11 into his high school years. After my work with the Forest Service, I eventually got a job with the Idaho Employment Department in Salmon. Mat would go to his friend Johnny's house after school. After I got off work at 5:00 I would pick up him up there. One winter night, after reaching North Fork, we decided it would be best to chain up before we proceeded down the ice-and-snow-covered Salmon River Road. (One must realize that not only did the road have a solid sheet of ice underlayment that night, in addition it was all too common to find big rocks blocking one or both lanes or to come upon a herd of deer slipping and sliding in slow motion trying to avoid being hit. All these perils, combined with the Salmon River paralleling every twist and turn of the road, made for a harrowing drive. (In fact, Mat and I used to drive that road in the winter with our seat belts unhooked because we didn't want to be trapped in the car if it went in the river!) After we got to Indian Creek, we had to dig our way up one mile of ranch road! Jack had plowed two miles down from the upper gate. We were driving a late model Audi sedan at that point. Mat would get out and dig about a 20 or so foot stretch and I would inch forward. And so it went, dig, repeat, dig, repeat. Plus, there was no way to let anyone know where we were in our journey and when we would be home. To say we were drained of all physical energy when we got home doesn't begin to describe the exhaustion we felt. And that was day after day. However, I'm so glad that I had Mat with me.

There's no way I would have been able to make that repeated journey without him.

During one bitter winter, despite running our tap each night, our above-ground water line froze all the way back to its spring source. Oh it was great fun. Bernie had to haul each section of the frozen pipe into our (my) kitchen, wrapping it in a circular fashion reaching from the floor to the log ridge pole in our vaulted ceiling. We had to fire up the wood cook stove in order to thaw each section out. As each section thawed, we would drag the line out to the yard and shake out the ice chunks and reattach them. And so it went section by section. Like I said, fun! Bernie devised a solution though. He routed the incoming supply line with a T-connection that had a diverter valve, thus allowing a larger stream of incoming water to be diverted via a short garden hose back out to the exterior. That was such a blessing! In fact all the water mains in Salmon froze that winter and the residents were without running water for a month!

Another winter, he needed to repair the snow machine. And given that there was no source of heat in the barn, he *naturally* dragged it into the kitchen and, you guessed it, tore the engine apart and reassembled it. If memory serves me correctly, I believe that machine was in MY kitchen for over a week!

During every other season except the winter months, we kept our game meat (venison, elk & steel head trout) & meals I had cooked ahead in two lockers in Salmon. During the winter with a tiny refrigerator freezer and access out of the canyon limited, we had to get creative with storing our food for long periods. We placed a cooler in a snow bank outside the kitchen and stored frozen meat & veggies in it. We also used the snow banks to freeze gallons of milk. Miraculously those stores were never raided by a wild animal.

The following description coming from a winter's day walk toward the Jack and Lois's house is taken from a Christmas letter I wrote a few years ago. I believe that it is a perfect note on which to end this chapter:

"…many years ago I was hiking down a mountain road pressed in silence by the heavy snows of winter to visit our neighbors who ran a guest ranch. As I came round the bend, the last quarter mile of flat road bordering their north pasture stretched before me. To my left, a spit-rail fence fronted by towering fir trees, their boughs laden in winter's robe; to my right, a rise of dense forest marching up the mountain side. This tunnel of white, pristine of movement prior to my presence, orchestrated a synchronized unloading of the overarching boughs, a hushed *whoof,* a cloud-storm of white, and it was over. I, being the sole witness, was left shrouded in wonder."

The cabin and bridge under snow

Snowmobile playtime at 7,000 ft

Sue Kozacek – teaching me to cross-country ski

Lois with Mickey & Nappy taking a winter's walk

WHERE'S THE ELK?

The following incident happened prior to our arrival in Idaho. It's one of the many humorous tales Jack would pull out of his hat at a moment's notice.

Elk hunting in the North Fork/Salmon regions of Idaho is no small feat. Each fall prior to hunting season, the elk move up in long trains from the valleys to more remote mountainous grounds, much of the time slipping over the continental divide into Montana. For the serious nonlocal hunter, he or she is well-disposed to hire a guide and pack in with a combination of mules and horses and set up camp for at least a week. And even at that, one considers themselves lucky even to see an elk, much less bag one.

One day during hunting season, a young man came driving up the three mile stretch of the rock-strewn jarring road of lower Indian Creek Ranch to the upper gate in a Volkswagen Beetle. He had his honey sitting beside him. He stopped when he saw Jack and called out the window, "Hey Mister, where's the elk?" Jack hollered back, "Oh, just go up the road apiece - you'll see 'em." The kid waved out the window and yelled back, "Thanks Mister," and drove away.

Jack chuckled and shook his head as he went about his work. He knew he had just pulled a funny one on the kid, given the elk's reclusive ways.

Well, it turned out that the joke was on Jack. A couple hours later he saw the kid heading back down the road towards the ranch, his honey right next to him, but this time with an elk wrapped around the back of his VW from door knob to door knob! The kid hollered out the window, "Thanks Mister, it was just like you said. I went up the road about a mile and a whole herd was standing in the middle of it. Well, thanks again! See ya!" And off he went. The hunt was over.

Jack pushed the rim of his hat up, scratched his forehead and watched as the kid, totally oblivious to his good fortune, merrily bumped down the canyon.

Upper gate at Indian Creek Ranch

ANTLERS

During the summer months, Jack's lower pastures became the home for some thirty odd horses and mules owned by an outfitter by the name of John Boucher. Now JB was practically a legend downriver, not because of anything particularly outstanding he had done, rather because he was a character. He was in his sixties and, allowing for his bow-legs, he measured about 5'8". He was gritty-tough, sinewy from head to toe; jean-and-boot clad, with a shock of white hair irreverently captured beneath a beat-up cowboy hat – irreverent hair framing an irreverent face, forever gruff as if nothing ever went his way. His deep set blue eyes, gauged one from beneath a pair of bushy white brows and thin lips which were framed by a handlebar moustache.

Every fall JB would round up his stock for the purpose of packing deer and elk hunters into the back country. On one such occasion he and a hired hand, a tobacco-chewing old fellow, were driving the herd up the canyon towards Jack's corral. The herd was kicking up a storm of dust making it difficult to see. The hand said, "JB, does one of yer mules have a pair of antlers?" JB glared at him, "Hell no I don't have any *#%@ mule with antlers! What in the Sam hell you been smokin'?" Unruffled, the old man, replied, "Whelp, ya do now."

JB continued to grumble and cuss under his breath all the way up the canyon, assured by the knowledge that his companion had lost his marbles. But life in all its sweet surprises had one in store for him. With the dust settling on the backs of the herd, there stood in the center of the corral a magnificent bull moose! Unfazed by the whole affair, he stood just long enough for JB to catch sight of him and mumble additional words of exclamation. Then, with the ease and elegance of a giraffe, he stepped over the fence and was gone.

Some lived out their lives nestled in those hills and hollows not for the sheer awe of it, for they had not eyes to see. Rather, something deep inside of them knew they couldn't fit in anywhere else.

Indian Creek Ranch corral & barn

THE RANCH

The bruising September clouds draped the canyon walls of Iron Creek as I waited in my government-issue Forest Service pickup for a rancher by the name of Roy Morris. He wanted me to mark for cutting an assigned number of lodge pole pine trees located on Salmon National Forest land adjacent to his property. This was the first time I had marked trees without a partner and for a private citizen. Given that I was still somewhat new to my position with the timber-thinning crews and green at remaining compassed on true north when mountains blanketed me on every side, I was feeling a few trepidations, and the ominous clouds hanging about did nothing to allay those fears. The thought of Lewis and Clark getting lost near here and practically starving to death did not help.

Soon after, however, Mr. Morris pulled beside me in his tan pickup truck, got out and said his hellos and asked if I would please follow him to his property. He was broad at the shoulder, chest and waist, but solid, and wore a large off-white cowboy hat, a pressed shirt and jeans. He turned onto a road that T'ed in from my left. The road gave indications of being abandoned – gutted from snowmelts, lightning quick washes and neglect; nature seemed poised to reclaim it as its own. Within two miles he pulled onto a steep berm which turned out to be the entrance to his ranch. This too seemed abandoned, overwhelmed by vegetation on all sides. He got out, opened the gate and waved me on through. As my truck haltingly made its way upwards, my tires slipping, grabbing, slipping, the road in front fell from view and I was greeted with a twisted tangle of brush brimming over the sides and top of the vehicle on the passenger side. Grinding in compound low gear, the truck crested the rise and brought the anticipated scene into view. I caught my breath; I knew to my core that the sight that lay before me and the entire hue of the day to which it was wedded would be forever crystallized in my mind. I beheld the picture-perfect setting artists strive to recreate of the romanticized version of the West. Remember those magazine ads at Christmas-time for Marlboro cigarettes, with the cowboy dragging his fresh-cut Christmas tree behind his horse toward a softly lit cabin nestled in a snow covered mountainous valley? Well, that was the cabin; that was the scene – minus the cowboy, his horse, his tree and his cigarette - at that moment.

The log cabin set in a bowl of a high valley; a split rail fence shielded the yard from the tramplings of grazing cattle and several tiers of pasture bunkered the scraping gunmetal grey peaks, which served as the backdrop on all sides for the rolling pastures and pockets of gold-leafed Aspen. As shreds of storm-laden clouds scattered about depositing their crystals, I caught glimpses of snowfields already entrapped in the cavities of the sheared ridges. The cabin lay low and wide and square, with a straight porch supporting a tin shed roof its entire length. Smoke lingered about the stove pipe, confused as to its course. It looked warm and inviting.

As we pulled up in front, we were greeted by a crusty old cowboy by the name of Jim. He was bone-thin, bow-legged and possessed a face time had chiseled its remembrances upon. His cowboy hat was weathered and sweat-stained and looked about as old and beat-up as he did. He was "mighty glad" to see us and offered some cowboy coffee to "warm-up our hides." (I'm not making this up.) The cabin consisted of one large room. I cannot recall the details except that the kitchen table sat in the center, with a wood heating stove close beside it. The room was spare, rough around the edges, but so was its occupant.

Jim's boss, Roy, was quite pleasant to me but seemed distant, almost wary (after all I was with the government), until it became readily apparent Jim and I had clicked with one another. We sat and chatted for about ten or so minutes. I remember discussing the weather and that Roy was going to take me to the far northwest corner of the ranch. Nothing earth-shattering was discussed, yet we laughed freely and without assumption. I believe Jim was as charmed by me as I was him, like opposite sides of the same coin; we wanted a taste of what the other's world was about. The occasion took on a glow, and I felt singularly blessed to have been afforded the honor to sit in the company of these two men. I can describe it no other way. In the coming years I would see Roy at the local hangout, the Salmon River Café, or at a dance in the attached bar, and he would always tip his hat. A chord had been struck that day and in the time-honored Western way, nothing further needed to be said.

We said our goodbyes to Jim and each got in our separate trucks. We drove through the far gate and headed up a dirt road toward a bench; pastures were scattered before us, some at higher elevations and some at a distance below. A riot of yellow Aspen seemed to greet us at every turn. Cattle looked up expectantly as we passed by. We negotiated several switchbacks, passed through gates, then additional switchbacks and gates until we found ourselves in a sea of golden grass with no visible road. I wished I could ask Roy to stop so I might drink in all that was about me in this exquisite high mountain valley – the pockets of shimmering Aspen set to the backdrop of shadowed pines and sheer rock faces. Like a movie set on fast-forward, the feel of it was changing before my eyes – the surreal light cast from inky tattered storm clouds was slipping away as the more ominous mother clouds overtook the sky.

We finally arrived on the far side of the field and were high enough now to be in a snowstorm. We hiked for about a mile up a thin trail that was flanked by tall dense timber on either side. I found my mind wandering to thoughts of bears and allowed an air of foreboding to prickle through me, as the thick heavy flakes kept coming down and the timber seemed to move closer the further up the trail we hiked. Roy located the pole patch and indicated the number of trees he wished me to mark. He said goodbye and threw over his shoulder that he hoped I could find my way back. *What????* I was devastated!! I had been so enraptured with the events of the day that I hadn't thought through why we had stayed in separate vehicles. I threw back, "Me too!" But in all actuality my heart had caught in my throat. I could only pray that my instincts would serve me well because my memory was filled with only fragments of our journey - an exquisite bunching of Aspen here or a feisty gate there, with a smattering of switchbacks thrown in for good measure.

Working fast, wanting to flee this place that threatened to swallow me up, I probably marked more trees than Roy dare hope for in his wildest dreams, causing him to be beholden to me for life. *Fine, that'll work; my only repayment need be full access to this ranch.* Two forces were at work within my psyche – fear, stretching her boney finger in and rattling it around, and peace, as encompassing as the umbrella of timbers which surrounded me. Nary a flitter was to be heard in the underbrush. Nothing – just the heavy silent flakes floating down.

Finally bumping into the orange flags tied to understory branches which delineated the stand's perimeter, my pace was quickened by the imagined bears peering at this intruder into their silent domain. Never mind that all such alleged bears were in hibernation – they were there and they were watching me! After leaping into the truck, slamming the door shut and locking it, I resolved to take the ranch one section at a time. The only difficulty was that the snow had become ponderous, destroying my visibility. I felt my way out of the high pasture and onto the appearance of a road, but as I was soon to discover, the road had been abandoned. I drove gingerly down several switchbacks, but large and jagged stones eventually made it impassable. I had no choice but to back out. This was no time for the faint-of-heart; I needed enough controlled power for the tires to grab, but giving it a burst of gas would have sent me over the edge into oblivion. Slow and steady, slow and steady, keeping my wits about me, I kept backing until a switchback afforded me enough room to turn the truck to rights and continue climbing until it hit level ground.

Acknowledging my total disorientation, I attempted to radio the Salmon Ranger station and report that I was lost. That was my lowest point; I needed to prove myself not only to my superiors and my co-workers but to myself as well. My husband had already dazzled them with his skills, enthusiasm and adaptability. Now here came his wife from "back East." *Would she prove to have the same metal or not?* I felt I had no choice – the situation warranted it. "Salmon 8, this is Marcia. Do you copy? Salmon 8, this is Marcia. Do you copy?" Trying to keep my voice calm, "Salmon 8, this is Marcia. Do you copy?" Nothing. NOTHING. I was out of range; I was on my own. Remember, one section at a time. Thank heavens, though barely visible, I managed to backtrack following the tire's imprints in the snow to the upper pasture. By then, sweet luck, the snow squall had abated and I discerned the faint outline of another track.

This led to another and another, each becoming more distinct as I made my way down; and the gates – those maddening gates: it was love at each sighting; and crisp golden leaves of the aspen, and the cows – those beautiful dumb beasts – impassively watching me pass by, until wonder upon wonders, I came upon the split rail fence framing the cabin! I was elated beyond measure.

I stopped to say goodbye to Jim as he came out on the porch, with that beat-all-to-hell cowpoke hat on, bare hands in his jean pockets and shoulders scrunched bracing against the high country air. "I thought ya might a lost yer way with that snow squall and all."

I grinned sideways with my forearm resting on the open window of the truck. "Yeah, it was a little tricky getting out of there, but I managed."

Yeah, you managed alright. But do you think you can manage to keep from jumping out of this truck and throwing your arms around him? Just the sight of a real live human being makes him look awfully pretty, doesn't it?

My first impression had been correct; the sights that I saw this day and my experiences with them would remain with me forever; but on a much deeper level, a solid timber to my soul had been tucked firmly into place.

SAFE IN THE BAG

John and Patti Hulihan were dear friends of ours who lived next to the Salmon River down river from Indian Creek. They had built a small log cabin at the base of Gold Hill Mines. Gold Hill Mine was an abandoned mining operation that still possessed the processing building and open mine shafts leading into the mountainside. John and Patti were wonderful people to be around, each possessing a zest for life and learning and a hearty sense of humor.

One evening they were driving down the river road when they spotted a very large rattlesnake. John did what he normally does in this situation. He retrieved his pistol from the glove compartment, got out of the truck and shot the snake through the head.* With Patti's assistance, he then placed it in a paper bag they happened to have handy. After getting back in the truck, with Patti holding the bag on her lap, they proceeded on down the road.

In the past, they would have tossed the snake to the side of the road, allowing it to become a feast for neighboring birds such as magpies, eagles and crows. However, Wes Dorman, the owner of the Shoup Store located about a mile up from the mine, had begun using rattlesnake skins to make hat bands and then selling them in the small general store. Every now and then John and Patty would bring him a rattler which had had the misfortune of crossing their path.

The Hulihans were about five miles upriver from Shoup when the bag came alive! The snake began flailing and gyrating about. Patti cried out, "Oh-h-h-h N-o-o-o!" She quickly rolled the top of the bag tighter and dropped it on the floor, not quite letting go. The last thing she wanted was for the bag to fall over and the snake to come crawling out. John hit the gas, and they were at Shoup in no time. As it was past closing, they took the sack and placed it on the back stoop with a note which read, "Snake inside. We THINK it's dead!!!" With their good deed done, they headed on down the road.

~

Rattlesnakes are viewed as a menace in this part of the country. They reside in overwhelming numbers as their natural predators are on the decline. John and Patti did not participate in the hunting of any game and did what they could to aid in its preservation. However, as a matter of survival, John commonly carried a pistol when they hiked or traveled the river road.

John and Patti

Idaho Timber Rattlesnake

SHADOW

I arrived home after dark after a long, grueling ten-hour day working for the Forest Service. My only wishes were to finish off the last piece of quiche, wash myself, and snuggle in for a good read before I dozed off to sweet slumber. I had just arranged myself on the couch when a dark form, given to flight, brushed by my head and was silently absorbed into the shadowy recesses of the room. In that split second in which the mind must assimilate reality in order to take action, I faintly drew in my breath and froze, then shook it off. Surely this was my imagination – the cabin was absolutely still. If something was looming about, there would be sounds. And with these comforting thoughts, I continued reading. Alas, the next fly-by left no doubt as to the identity of my eerie friend – a BAT! I had a BAT in my cabin, at night, while I was alone!!! In addition, I could barely make it out because our only lighting was by means of propane wall lamps. Not good.

This was simply too much for a novice mountain woman such as me to handle. I flew to the phone and rang Jack. I just knew there would be no question – he would immediately come up the canyon and do something! I called out, "Jack, there is a bat in my cabin!" To my horror he replied, "I'll tell ya what ya do..." That's what he said, *I'll tell ya what 'you' do!!*

After I argued and pleaded and finally, in submission, thanked him, I hung up the receiver, took a deep breath and got a broom and paper sack. I waited, broom cocked over my heat near my foe's flight path. It didn't take long – the soundless creature was before me. I whacked him to the floor, stunning him, then quickly covered him with the sack and slipped the newspaper beneath to lift him up. Without further hesitation I was to the door, setting my intruder free. I slammed the door shut, jumped into bed and sat there in wide-eyed wonder at the fact, everything was okay – I had handled the situation just fine. One part of me saying, *Alright, good job lady!* And then dumbfounded relief took possession and I fell into a sweet numbing slumber.

Me, under less stressful conditions

LONE ELK

One bright crisp fall day as we hunted on the mountainsides behind our cabin for antlers that had been dropped by deer or elk the preceding spring, Bernie came upon a young bull elk standing about 20 feet from a place where he had apparently been bedded down for quite some time. I say apparently because the earth was padded down and wreaked of urine. Bernie called to me, and as I approached, the young bull remained standing in place, looking at us with a combination of fear and sadness emanating from his eyes. We noticed that a joint on one of his front legs was quite swollen. This explained why he had been bedded down in the same spot – the leg was injured enough to incapacitate him.

We called Russ Kozacek, the Fish and Game Warden, and asked that he determine if the elk had any chance of survival given his injury. Russ hiked up the mountainside with a pistol in hand assuming that he would need to put the animal down. However, after studying his wound, he decided that the elk's leg was healing and said if we would be willing to provide him with water and hay and hay pellets over the winter, he might survive until the following spring. That was if a coyote or mountain lion or bobcat didn't come upon him in the meantime.

So began a commitment on the part of Bernie to haul feed and water up the mountainside to this vulnerable elk. The animal would call out in a high-pitched squeal at Bernie's approach and then become silent as he came near.

About a month after we first discovered this young bull, a string of elk passed near our cabin as they moved to higher ground for the winter. As the injured bull started whistling to them, they would whistle back. And so it went calling to each other back and forth until their calls became so faint as to be heard no more. The young bull kept calling long after their response had died away. It was the most haunting event I became party to while in Idaho – leaving me with a hollow ache in my heart.

After many weeks of loyally feeding our patient, Bernie didn't hear the familiar whistle as he approached with hay and water. The young bull was gone. Bernie looked for signs of blood and bones but found nothing to indicate that the elk had been attacked by a predator. By all appearances, he had healed enough to rejoin his herd. We felt such a sense of relief and outright joy thanks to a providential set of circumstances that had allowed this young bull to live.

Injured bull elk

WHEN MORSE CODE FAILS

It was an unassuming building built of lap-board cedar stained dark brown with a shed porch roof running its length. During warmer months its eve was heavy with hanging bleeding-heart baskets alight with warring hummingbirds. An oversized pine bench sat beneath the café windows, with the requisite ice machine in front of the attached general store. To the store's right could be found the restrooms and two pay phones. Though casual in appearance it may have been, this was the gathering and supply place for the locals living in this remote region of Idaho. This was especially so for those living off the 30 mile stretch of the Salmon River Road where electricity cut off beyond North Fork and phone service was still in the form of crank phones. Even though this was in the early 1980's, the residents downriver would have it no other way. The café and store was also the local hub for tourist traffic, whether they be steelhead fishermen, river rafters, or hunters. This was the North Fork General Store & Café, owned by Ken and Diane with their partner, Don. Well run, yes, however serving as an outpost as it was, they allowed the local flavor of the waitresses' personalities full expression.

On this particular morning, Ken could stand it no more – his muscles were knotted across his upper back and he'd even taken to snapping at his wife Diane – a line he rarely crossed. He needed a break – too many things to juggle as of late, what with the summer river rafting traffic soon to shift into high gear. The idea lit and immediately caused his blood pressure to drop to a reasonable level. He would isolate himself in the basement, just for the afternoon. No one would miss him and he could play in his long abandoned workshop.

He had a wonderful day enjoying the feel of the tools in his hands once again. The waitresses and customers alike grew used to his erratic hammering below. Everything was going fine, that is, until Darlene, the cook, went to the freezer, located in the basement, and on her way out inadvertently locked the exterior door hatch. In defense of Darlene, that rote act had been drilled into all employees from the get-go.

Soon thereafter, Ken, highly satisfied with his accomplishments and feeling almost buoyant, decided to call it a day and return to work. He went to the only means of egress and soon learned his fate. Ken was not happy, especially not being disposed to a light heart by nature. In fact, Ken was one whose brows were forever knotted. It was difficult to understand why – he and Diane were living their dream. No matter, his brows were knotted as usual and, being the logical person he was, decided to communicate his predicament to his staff via tapping the Morse code signal for S.O.S. on the floor joists below the restaurant. It wasn't even on his radar that they wouldn't immediately hone in on the signal and he would be out in no time. I fear his logic failed to consider the staff at hand – all young females, born and raised in the immediate region, leaving them void of any exposure to signal training. Instead, they simply went about their business waiting tables, filling orders, and joking with the locals that Ken must be having a good time down there… banging-away!

No one really knows how long Ken attempted rescue via this method because he never wanted to talk about the incident afterwards. One can only surmise his thought process as he took stock of his situation – numerous people above, him isolated below. Obviously realizing his first efforts were in vain – after all a rescue party had not arrived in short order. He must devise a more straightforward means of communication. Soon thereafter, a young couple eating dinner in a small half-walled-off room towards the back of the restaurant noticed a slip of paper attached to a crude wire being pushed through the floor heating grate. As the wire lazily floated around, the young man pulled the paper off and found a note which read, "HELP, I'M LOCKED IN THE BASEMENT!" (Do I dare ask what his initial thoughts might have been, passing through this remote region as they were, and stumbling upon this desperate plea for help? *What sinister thing could be happening here? Should I unobtrusively call the sheriff, or pass a note to the party below asking what is going on, or dare let the manager know that the gig is up and their captive is about to bust free?)*

Well, nothing that dramatic happened, but you might imagine the commotion when news of Ken's predicament reached his staff. Everyone was running around bumping into each other talking all at once saying, Oh, my gosh, how long has he been down there? *Oh, my gosh, I'm not going to get him – he'll be livid!* Even Diane refused to go! Finally, one of the waitresses, Jack and Lois's daughter Theresa, said she would go. She went down, unlocked the door, stepped back and let Ken out. Well, Ken came out all right – stormed out, without a word. In fact he did not mention the subject for over a week and heaven knows everyone about him didn't dare broach the subject. It must be told though, the story somehow found its way into every hill and holler within fifty miles up and down the neighboring corridor, causing belly-aching laughter at the thought of Ken, flailing a note around the restaurant.

Ultimately Bernie and I could stand it no more. We rigged up a phone system to be used by the restaurant and personally delivered it to Ken in a shoebox. We explained that we had heard that he had been having trouble communicating with his employees and we simply wanted to help out. He opened the box and in it he found two tin cans strung together with a piece of yarn. On one can were the words, "TALK HERE," and on the other, "LISTEN HERE." One corner of his mouth slipped into a grin, and he asked if we would like a refill on our coffees.

North Fork General Store & Café'

LOIS DOES IT HER WAY

One night while Jack and Lois were peaceably sleeping, they were shocked awake by shattering glass in their kitchen. Their dog Nappy led the way, being restrained by Jack's firm hold on his collar. With flashlight in hand they crept down the hallway single-file toward a loud smacking noise. Directing the beam around the pitch-black kitchen, Jack froze when the light located a 300 lb. bear sitting on their side counter eating the chocolate sponge cake Lois had baked fresh that day! A low-throated growl came from Nappy, and his body tensed into a stealth-like crouching mode, straining Jack forward.

One might suspect any range of emotions being felt by the Jack and Lois at that moment, primary among them – fear. But necessity dictated different reactions, leaving no place for such. Their very remoteness didn't allow for the possibility of calling the humane society or police to inform them that there was a bear in their kitchen and would they please come and remove him. A fish and game warden did live up-river if they could only get to their phone. However, this would have involved cranking the phone in order to ring the operator and then shouting into the mouthpiece regarding their unfortunate situation – not a wise choice under the circumstances. By then the cake would have been gone, but not the bear.

Jack was a logical, practical man, used to these untimely adventures with wildlife. He knew that bears do not usually exit the same way they enter. Well, one can only imagine.... He said, "Lois, I think we had better let Nappy take care of this one." But Lois was not thinking of practicality. She was furious, but not about the cake. The cake had nothing to do with it! She was furious because THAT BEAR had broken her prized cake stand! There it lay, shattered on the floor, with THAT BEAR sitting on HER counter, EATING! She grabbed the flashlight from Jack and charged him waving it wildly and shouting, "You get out of my kitchen! Now get!" The bear didn't have time to think of an elaborate means of escape. His only thought was getting away from the wild banshee charging him. One turn and he was out the window with Nappy leaping onto the counter barking ferociously after him. Lois turned to look at Jack.

Jack just kept scratching his head, "Lois, what the HELL were ya thinking? That's not how to talk to a bear!"

"Well that's how I talk to a bear, and HE LISTENED!"

o argument there, Lois.)

BIG MOTH

One evening around dusk, Jack and Lois were having dinner with paying guests. It was a pleasant evening, with a mild passing breeze. The nights had finally held the warmth of the day enough that Jack was able to remove the plastic sheeting from the windows, leaving screens over the openings on three sides of the room. The room can be likened to a very large screened in porch (20' X 40'). It had a dining table running half the length of one long wall, with a piano and primitive style hutch opposite, and a pair of log love seats and tables at the far end of the room. The dining area overlooked a large wrap-around porch with a ponderosa pine tree housed within its perimeters.

Having spent many a pleasant evening seated at that table, I was all too aware of the fact that a person could reach a state of bliss within themselves. One felt they must have arrived in paradise. The calls of the fast-paced world were but whispers, competing with the soft night air

95

carrying with it the abundant scent of pine and sounds of the evening birds and horses neighing in the corral below. One became entranced with Jack and Lois sharing their array of magical stories of former guests and adventures.

It was at this internal state that an older couple had arrived when a very large winged shadow drifted over their heads and disappeared into the kitchen. The woman said, "WHAT was that?" Never batting an eye, Lois replied in her sweet high pitched voice, "A big moth." In truth, it was a bat, and Lois knew it, but heaven forbid she should allow the guests to know it. City folk, especially those from "back-East" (anyone living west of the Rockies), had a particularly difficult time dealing with some of the realities life had to offer in this remote mountainous region. Best to break them in as gently as possible, and Lois was a master of the task. "Jack, why don't you see where it went?" Jack got up and soon found the bat in the bathroom. He casually retrieved a broom, returned to the bathroom and shut the door. After a few thunderous thuds – WHACK, WHACK, WHACK – Jack returned to the dinner table and quietly resumed eating. The guests didn't ask, and Jack didn't offer. The enchanted evening continued.

OPERATOR

Lois rang to say Mary had called so I headed down the canyon to call her back. Mary, I missed her dearly and we had much catching up to do. Living in the suburbs of Kansas City, she delighted in imagining the characters and events which now filled my life. It seemed every time she went through the challenging process of attempting to ring Indian Creek Ranch a fun event was in store for her.

When I reached her, she said her first hurdle was to convince the on-line operator that she needed to get in touch with someone who was still on an old "ring down" line. The operator asked what she meant, and Mary explained that the party she wished to reach had a crank style phone. The operator replied that that style was out of existence in the United States and would she please offer a correct number. Mary explained, "I realize this doesn't make sense to you but the phone system does exist and I have reached this party before at this number. The number is

24F-211, the last three numbers stand for two longs, one short and one long." At this point a supervisor was called in and Mary explained that she simply needed to be put in touch with a Salmon, Idaho operator because that operator had the equipment necessary to ring the party in question. Mary could provide the routing if they wished. The supervisor agreed and then Mary read aloud from the instructions I had sent her, Routing 208 plus 057 plus 121. Mark 208-996.

Voila', a ring was heard, then a voice, "Salmon." And from the on-line operator, "Operator, we have a party wishing to reach someone at a ring down number?" The Salmon operator replied, "Yes." Mary thought, *Finally!* However the operator said, "The downriver line is busy." Mary said, "May I hold?" The operator said yes she could but she must realize there were 22 parties on that line and someone could ring out at any time. Mary held anyway. In about ten minutes the operator said, "Ringing." However, there was tremendous crackling on the line.

Mary said, "We seem to have a bad connection. May we try again?" The operator said, "Oh honey, it's always like that. The line is strung over the mountains and rock outcroppings and through sage brush. This is as good as you're going to get." Mary was laughing by the time Lois answered, "Indian Creek Ranch." Mary said this was Marcia's friend Mary and where in the world did we really live? She felt as though it must be on a different planet. Lois laughed and said sometimes she had wondered herself. She said she would ring me and I would hike down the canyon to call back. If the line was not tied up it would be about thirty minutes. She also told Mary she was glad she called because it gave her a good excuse to have morning tea with me.

This day it worked out and I was able to get right back in touch with Mary. We had a lovely visit. I am just glad that she had the persistence to keep in touch with me fairly regularly during my Idaho years and would put up with having to speak with a raised voice. She always sounded a million miles away, and I sometimes imagined we were living in parallel universes and were only able to talk between them by means of a tin-can phone system. Without really discussing it, she was able to remind me of who I was and what I was about. With Mary there needn't be any explanations because we went so far back together. It was comforting – kind of like touching base or returning home.

CHASE

It had been a common morning – breakfast, followed by early morning chores of feeding her menagerie of pets, then menu planning for paying guests due to arrive at their guest ranch by week's end. Deciding to take a break, Lois found herself cozied up on her couch, gazing down the canyon as she warmed herself with a soothing cup of hot tea. She watched with mild interest as her Jeep Cherokee was driven from its parking spot in back of her ranch house to the split rail pasture gate below. She saw the gate swing open; the Jeep drive through and stop on its far side; the gate close and the Jeep proceed at a leisurely pace down the three mile stretch of the dusty ranch road toward the lower ranch gate, ultimately exiting onto the Salmon River Road. A clear view of the entire event was not afforded her because a large Douglas-fir obstructed her line of sight. No matter, she was not concerned – it was just their daughter, Theresa, using Lois's car to drive to work.

Not concerned, that is, until a few moments later Theresa walked into the adjacent kitchen to get breakfast. Lois called out, "What are you doing here? You just left for work."

"No, I just got up."

"No you didn't."

"Yes, I did."

"Then who just drove my car down the canyon?"

Such was the start to a day which when retold in the years to come would sound as if it were lifted from a script for the *Dukes of Hazard*. This was to be high adventure in North Fork.

Lois immediately phoned the sheriff in Salmon to report her Jeep Cherokee being stolen. With no more to be done, Theresa reluctantly left for the North Fork Cafe' where she was a waitress. Before leaving though, she slipped a small derringer into her purse. The North Fork Cafe' was located at the intersection of Highway 93 (which travels north to Lost Trail Pass and south to the town of Salmon) and the Salmon River Road. Upon Theresa's arrival with the news of the stolen vehicle, everyone was keeping an eye peeled for the stolen Jeep.

Apparently when the stolen vehicle had reached the base of Indian Creek Ranch, it had turned west on the Salmon

River Road, unwittingly missing the sheriff who arrived about 20 minutes later from the opposite direction. While the sheriff was interviewing Lois at the ranch house, the Jeep's occupants, realizing that the area was becoming more primitive the further downriver they drove, turned around and headed toward North Fork, passing the entrance to Indian Creek Ranch in so doing.

Shortly thereafter, as Theresa was waiting a table, shouts began coming from the front counter, "Theresa, there goes your mom's Jeep!!" Theresa looked out to see the Cherokee slowly pull up to the stop sign where the river road "T"s" into Highway 93, then slowly pull out and head south toward Salmon. Theresa grabbed her purse and jumped into her car, signaling her departure trailing gravel and dust into the air, and vanished in pursuit. Once on the highway, she glanced in her rear view mirror discovering Ken, her boss, was providing her with backup by following in his car.

Within moments Theresa was upon the unsuspecting thieves. They had continued poking along until her menacing green vehicle loomed large in their rear view mirror. The chase was on! They whipped a "U," hit the accelerator and headed for Lost Trail Pass and the Montana border.

Theresa and Ken followed suit, each squealing their tires, throwing dust and gravel off the shoulders. Ken soon passed Theresa, elbows locked, hands gripping the wheel, determined not to let the suspects get away. One must understand, these were all older model cars – the stolen car, an o-l-d Jeep Cherokee; Theresa's, a Pontiac Lemans (aka, the Green Bomb); and Ken's Toyota Corolla (one of the original?) – each being strained to its limits. In fact, the Cherokee was careening over the center line as it raced up the two-lane winding highway.

With Ken right on the tail of the Jeep, the passenger rolled into the back seat, grabbed a rifle and pointed it at Ken. Ken kept his foot on the gas and with one hand on the wheel, reached behind his bucket seat and pulled out the first object his hand landed on – a tire iron. Bringing it to bear with forthright determination, he rested the horizontal crossbar between two fingers of his left hand (the one holding the steering wheel) while gripping the lower half of the vertical "T" with his right hand, and took aim at his adversary, never flinching at the stakes. The boy ducked down and hid from view, probably yelling, "Faster!" to the driver.

While this drama unfolded up Hwy 93, the switchboard in Salmon was lit up like a Christmas tree with reported sightings of the stolen vehicle up and down river: *I saw Lois's Jeep do a "U" turn downriver at Shoup and head toward North Fork! It's headed into Salmon! No, it's headed toward Lost Trail Pass with Theresa and Ken in pursuit!*

As the freewheeling convoy passed through the tiny town of Gibbonsville, a doddering old man was approaching the road to get his mail. First one car zoomed by, then another, then a third, with a woman yelling from its window, "CALL THE COPS!!!" He seemed to stand there in a daze, transfixed. The race continued, each car straining more as the assent to the pass began.

As the first switchback came into view, the thieves spun into a "U" shaped turn-around. Ken slammed on his brakes and yanked his steering wheel first to the right then to the left, throwing his car into a sideways skid before coming to a halt, thus effectively blocking one exit. Theresa followed Ken's lead by racing to the other exit and bringing her car to a stop in a broadside position. Before Theresa could get out, the two bandits had jumped out of Cherokee and were heading for the thickly timbered mountains of the Continental Divide. Ken had leapt out of his car and planted himself in a firing stance with his legs spread, arms outstretched, and right hand resting in the palm of his left. With his index finger outstretched, he took aim and yelled with the authority of a man with unquestionable firepower, "STOP, OR I'LL BLOW YOUR GUTS OUT!!" One boy dropped his rifle and threw up his arms. The other took flight in the forest. Theresa moseyed over to Ken and slipped him the derringer saying, "You might want this."

Shortly thereafter the sheriff was in his personal truck following the route of Ken and Theresa when he offered a teenage hitchhiker a ride. Within moments of getting in the cab the boy realized his mistake – he was in the hands of the law.

And so ended the teenage bandits' joy ride, but not without damage to the Cherokee. The culprits had rolled the car down a ravine before heading for the hills, thus bending the frame and throwing various other parts out-of-whack. The boys eventually paid restitution as well as serving time. It is an understatement to say that after this incident, the folks in the North Fork region viewed Ken and Theresa in a whole new light.

HUBCAPS AND DIGNITY

Given that our vehicles traveled rough roads on a daily basis, we were always minus a few hubcaps at any given time. I never paid it much mind when I was downriver. However, if I found myself running errands in Salmon, that was a whole different matter – these were town folk and I had my dignity to attend to. I therefore placed the two remaining hubcaps on the same side of the car. Hence, if I passed someone in town on the hubcap side, I would smile and wave. However, if they were on the opposite side of my car, I just held my head up and kept driving! As I'm quite sure you understand, in such a case there was absolutely no need to call unnecessary attention to myself.

THE END, NOT THE END

As I've recalled my experiences in Idaho, I've come to realize how deeply that life shaped the person I am today. I was given party to encounters with nature and wild animals that most can only read about or experience through film. I had the privilege of working alongside strong, capable women who, after taking my measure, accepted me as equal. Even though this was not like a Bear Grylls survival story, each day presented something unexpected; after all, we worked in the forest among its inhabitants. It kept one's senses on alert taking in all necessary information.

It took me many years after my parents died to realize that they were traveling along with me, in that all the love and instruction they had poured into me had literally become a part of who I am. My parents are in me; I can feel them in my soul! The same is true with all that I encountered while out west. Most of the stories I have recounted are light-hearted or informative in nature. I chose not to offer an analysis of how I grew from the young woman who could see all shades of grey and left the important decisions to others, into the person who emerged on the far side of this adventure offering anything but that. By then I knew what I stood for and what was worth fighting for. I had become comfortable in my own skin sans the need for self-analysis books. For me that knowledge came by way of firsthand experience bit by precious bit, until it was part of my timber.

As with any of life's journeys, what we experience comes to make up who we are and the reservoir we have to draw upon as we go forward. I think because I experienced an idyllic childhood full of adventures exploring the fields and woods and streams right out our backdoor in a small Missouri town, I was primed to eventually step forward from fear and loneliness to greet the wonder which was before me. The relaxed Zen-like pace of life at our home in the mountains and awareness of our surroundings required in performing our jobs for the Forest Service allowed me to notice and be open to the unexpected experiences which might greet me on any given day. I wanted to recall so many of those side events during my story-telling but felt it would detract from the tale at hand. In closing, I'd like to share a few of them.

On occasion I drove to Missoula, Montana for a day with friends. On this particular bitter winter's day it was Sue at the wheel and Tim (a Range Conservationist like Sue with the BLM) and me as passengers. We had had a grand time eating fine food and shopping a bit downtown and were headed home. It was around 10:00 P.M. when we arrived at the snow-covered summit of Lost Trail Pass. The highway was clear so we weren't experiencing any problems there. The problem presented itself in the form of a healthy looking beagle by the side of the road. Naturally we stopped and were able to coax him into the backseat next to Tim. The dog had a small plastic barrel attached to his collar with a note inside indicating where he lived. Great! The problem was that he lived at the base of Lost Trail Pass in Montana – on the road we had just travelled! Of course we moaned yet chuckled and turned around to take our new occupant home. What made it funny was that our 'friend' didn't want to have anything to do with us! He turned his back to Tim, put his nose in the air and ignored him the whole way down! I could almost read his thoughts: *Why do I have to suffer my presence with these strange people!!* Thirty minutes later we found his home, a ranch house tucked against the mountainside a fair ways off the highway. With the dog in his arms Tim knocked on the door near midnight! The kind rancher greeted him and was most grateful for our efforts. Our good deed was done with miles to go before we slept. Yet, it was worth it. Even though our passenger may have been ungrateful, he kept his dignity and allowed us without incident to return him to the safety of his home.

As I have mentioned, mostly I worked on Stand Exam in the company of women. Many times we would travel in a cumbersome extended cab truck, lacking power steering, which we called a six-pack. In the early '80's all-wheel drive had not come into existence, and a person couldn't simply hit a switch to engage all four wheels. Whenever we encountered snow-covered or slick roads, someone would have to get out and turn a lever of sorts on the wheels. They were extremely difficult to turn, especially when coupled with snow and freezing temperatures; one just had to grit their teeth and do it. A few times it was necessary to change a tire on a narrow logging road – in the snow of course!! This was dangerously difficult and unnerving but a task we managed as a team. Some units were such a distance from the ranger station that it conserved time for us to camp and work four ten-hour days. Most of these women were health-oriented and gourmet cooks. We had an arrangement that each of us was responsible for one meal while camped. Let me tell you, we ate well. The benefits were many. On rare occasions one team or another was treated to a mountain slope completely filled with blooming Sego Lilies (the bulb like roots were considered a delicacy by Native Americans), or Arrowleaf Balsamroots, or Indian Paintbrush or Bear Grass in a sparsely timbered area.

Sometimes a new crew member was added to Stand Exam. When that happened this person would temporarily be placed on an existing crew until they became comfortable with the protocols required. On one occasion, a botanist by the name of Robert was assigned to our crew. Robert always donned a red work vest and a yellow hard hat. The thing about Robert was that he was continually mesmerized by plant life we would come across as we trekked from one plot to another. I would be far into my paces only to find Robert well behind, bent down examining a plant that had nothing to do with the information we were to collect. We constantly had to yell, "Robert! Come on! You're slowing us up!" And Robert might reply, "Yes, but look, it's a Lady's Fairy Slipper!" One time I looked back in time to see a hummingbird that mistakenly thought Robert was a very large flower because of his red vest and yellow hat! It flew right up to his face and kept buzzing up and down and round and round in front of him. With his eyes wide open, Robert's head was bopping around and up and down trying to follow the hummer. It was hysterical, each in a state of total confusion!!

Another time a man by the name of Steve was assigned to me for a short period. We had pulled the truck up to an open patch which was part of our unit. As we were making ready to get out, a doe ran from the timber on our right, across the open area and disappeared into the timber on our left. Moments later she was trailed by a coyote. Just as we started to exit our truck again, the coyote shot out of the timber being chased by the doe!!! It was wonderful! I was yelling, "You go girl!"

Even though we lived in a remote area, residents downriver from North Fork and up toward Lost Trail Pass (encompassing about a 50 mile stretch) were a community of sorts. The North Fork Café was a true gathering place for the locals (and tourists too during their season). For the locals though, there was always a lot of jawing going on when we saw one another in the café and store. During the winter months we would meet to play cribbage either at the café after hours, or at the Jack and Lois's ranch or at the unused school house in Gibbonsville (a small town at the base of Lost Trail Pass). I wish I was able to gather the words to communicate how special it was to be a part of this band of independent souls who came from all walks of life yet formed a loose-knit union with each other. The unwritten code was, live and let live. We had come from "back East" and yet became accepted as one of their own. I am still humbled by that.

One thing I will never forget – the stars – the stars were like big fat diamonds, gazillions of them, so close, just a touch away. When I would look up on a clear night sky, I had to wonder with beauty such as this, how could there be any evil and hate and wretchedness in the world – it just seemed fathomless from that perspective, and it made my heart ache.

Sometimes in the summer we would raft the Salmon River. Even though it sounds benign, it was terrifying – to me at least. People had lost their lives rafting the stretches we routinely floated. The most dangerous rapid was the first one we encountered – Pine Creek. We would put in in calm water around the base of our canyon and gradually float to just above its deafening roar, positioning our raft in the most opportune fashion to make it through without tipping over. Once, our raft flipped at a 90-degree angle and dumped everyone out except for an eight-year-old boy and then, thank goodness, floated calmly into an eddy next to the shore.

On other days, we would tube the river and take out well above Pine Creek. It was unnerving enough to hear its roar in the distance. Tubing was more in tune with the speed I liked to experience the river. It was so tranquil and provided a respite from the heat of the day. When the river was low and running slow, usually by September, we were able to angle over to the far shore and visit friends. Those were the truly hearty folk. Since the road didn't run to their homes, they used a cable car(t) to get back and forth (carrying groceries, furniture, pets and whatnot). It basically consisted of a wooden tray hung from a steel cable which was strung from bank to bank. Pulley type wheels sat on top of the cable and the rider had to pull him or herself along by grabbing the cable hand over hand. A few riders lost a finger or two in the process. I never had a desire to try that mode of transport. Rather, I waited until September when I could grab my tube and coast over.

Bernie and I had a son while in Idaho. Not to worry, I didn't give birth under some pine tree and give him a weird name. No, our son Casey was born in the hospital in Salmon, thoroughly well-attended by a proper doctor. By that time, Bernie and Mat had built a log home on four-acres of pasture which we had purchased with the help of Jack from his cousin who owned the parcel. When our son was about a month old, I put him in a front pack and decided to walk up the road towards the ranch house. To my utter amazement, a herd of about ten horses interrupted their grazing and started following us at very close range; so close that I could feel their breath on my neck! They kept sniffing at Casey – this newborn. I had walked up that road many a time and the horses paid no attention to me. I've often wondered, what scent was it that they picked up, from across the field no less! The scent must have been similar to that of a newborn foal; why else would they be curious? It was both touching and totally unnerving!

Our marriage did come to an end, but not our friendship. Remarried, my husband Dean and I now live in the Kansas City area and Bernie lives in Denver with his wife. In fact, I have collaborated a bit with Bernie when writing this. His memory comes through when mine has failed and vice versa. Which is the point – yes, our lives together in that remote region of Idaho came to a close, but to paraphrase, "…look what I found along the way." And I've lived such a full life since, drawing on the deep well of resources that had become mine. Up until then I had spent my young adult life feeling like I was climbing a mountain, reading self-help books trying to understand myself. Back in Olathe, my professional career was made to order for me – being a facilitator in helping people rehab their homes and sometimes in that process, their lives. But, personally I was still searching until I arrived out West. No time to read self-help books out there! Somehow, as life often does, if we're willing to give it a chance and be patient with the process, the tumblers fall quietly into place. I left able to look anyone in the eye with both feet planted firmly on the ground. And life, in all its sweet surprises, brought me Dean. Looking back now, I do believe he was heaven sent.

Necessity dictated the means for transporting one's groceries & supplies across the Salmon River. (At left – manual cable cart)

114

Me with Sue Kozacek

Jack, making an art of relaxation

Epilogue

When Casey was seven, Dean and I decided that it was time to introduce him to some of the people and places in Idaho that he had heard so much about. The region and my friends did not disappoint. Prior to us heading home, he wrote to his teacher that he had panned for gold, blown up dynamite in a mine shaft, rafted the Salmon River, rode a horse, learned to shoot a bb gun and was called "deadeye," saw a rattlesnake, went irrigating with Jack on his motorcycle, and carved his initials in a tree on Indian Creek Ranch. Following is a composite of photos sharing some of those adventures and the dear people associated with them.

Casey & Jack

Jack and Casey ready to "irritate" (irrigate)

Jack shows Casey how to shoot - the making of a deadeye

*Theresa, Dean, me, Buckles (Casey's constant companion), Casey &
Jack*

Casey in the saddle

Casey & John setting dynamite in the Gold Hill Mine

Casey with John & Patti

Casey & Dean in an "intense" game of Mancala

Casey & me staffing John's photo stand

Casey at the Shoup Store, just up the road from the Gold Hill Mine

"Gold!"

Jack feeding Jack's horses

Marcia feeding Jack's horses

Casey feeding Jack's horses

ACKNOWLEDGMENTS

As I began the journey of writing this book I naively assumed that it would be my effort alone which would bring it to fruition. How silly of me.

As with most of the endeavors I have undertaken since I married you my dear, gentle and immensely talented husband Dean, you have provided the wings, if you will, by means of moral support, insights and use of your left brain to bring the raw material into publishable form.

Then we have Casey, the instigator. Thank you dear son for coming into my life and bringing with you unbounded joy, creativity, laughter, intelligence, and curiosity. After your nudging over the years I finally began putting pen to paper, thinking my sole motivation was to produce this book for you. It remained so, except that the actual process turned out to be a gift to myself. I discovered, as I believe you knew I would, that I do so love to write. Thank you. And thank you for your insightful edits to the final draft.

I am especially grateful to my dearest friend extraordinaire, Mary B., for your unflagging support and editorial expertise. I shudder to think what the end result would have been without your enthusiastic willingness to greet my ad nauseam requests to view each revision. I don't even wish to contemplate what my life's journey would have been like without you as my friend every step of the way. Besides my family, you have been one of my life's deepest gifts.

Marcia Katerndahl   2021

Front Cover: Marcia using a drawknife to manually shave bark off of future bridge logs
Back Cover: Salmon River at Indianola just above where it meets Indian Creek

Made in the USA
Coppell, TX
26 September 2021

MALPAUS WITH SHAHI RABADI

PHOTOGRAPHY BY JIGNESH JHAVERI